SpringerBriefs in Computer Science

SpringerBriefs present concise summaries of cutting-edge research and practical applications across a wide spectrum of fields. Featuring compact volumes of 50 to 125 pages, the series covers a range of content from professional to academic.

Typical topics might include:

- A timely report of state-of-the art analytical techniques
- A bridge between new research results, as published in journal articles, and a contextual literature review
- A snapshot of a hot or emerging topic
- An in-depth case study or clinical example
- A presentation of core concepts that students must understand in order to make independent contributions

Briefs allow authors to present their ideas and readers to absorb them with minimal time investment. Briefs will be published as part of Springer's eBook collection, with millions of users worldwide. In addition, Briefs will be available for individual print and electronic purchase. Briefs are characterized by fast, global electronic dissemination, standard publishing contracts, easy-to-use manuscript preparation and formatting guidelines, and expedited production schedules. We aim for publication 8–12 weeks after acceptance. Both solicited and unsolicited manuscripts are considered for publication in this series.

**Indexing: This series is indexed in Scopus, Ei-Compendex, and zbMATH **

Juan Fumero • Athanasios Stratikopoulos •
Christos Kotselidis

Programming Heterogeneous Hardware via Managed Runtime Systems

Springer

Juan Fumero
University of Manchester
Manchester, UK

Athanasios Stratikopoulos
University of Manchester
Manchester, UK

Christos Kotselidis
University of Manchester
Manchester, UK

ISSN 2191-5768 ISSN 2191-5776 (electronic)
SpringerBriefs in Computer Science
ISBN 978-3-031-49558-8 ISBN 978-3-031-49559-5 (eBook)
https://doi.org/10.1007/978-3-031-49559-5

This Springer imprint is published by the registered company Springer Nature Switzerland AG
The registered company address is: Gewerbestrasse 11, 6330 Cham, Switzerland

Paper in this product is recyclable.

Foreword by Monica Beckwith

The collective endeavor of Dr. Juan Fumero, Dr. Athanasios Stratikopoulos, and Dr. Christos Kotselidis in 'Programming Heterogeneous Hardware via Managed Runtime Systems' marks a pivotal achievement in the field of computing. Already deeply immersed in exploring JVM performance engineering and advanced hardware acceleration, my encounter with Dr. Juan's groundbreaking work at QCon London ignited a profound appreciation for his and his team's approach to TornadoVM, bridging the Java Virtual Machine (JVM) with exotic hardware accelerators. This appreciation further solidified upon delving into their comprehensive book.

Their work provides an insightful exploration of the evolving landscape of AI and heterogeneous computing, adeptly addressing the integration of dynamic programming languages within managed runtime environments (MREs) with the demands of hardware accelerators. The emphasis on General Purpose GPUs and their critical role in AI/ML workloads, is particularly compelling. TornadoVM, a focal point of this book, exemplifies this seamless integration of JVM with complex, heterogeneous environments.

Looking ahead, the manifold implications of their research paint a vivid picture of the future of computing. The book explores the nuanced integration of JIT-compiled code with pre-built kernels, illuminating a path where programming languages and exotic hardware accelerators not only coexist but also thrive in synergy. This evolution is further enhanced by significant advancements in memory management within the JVM. A key feature in this landscape is the development of the Foreign Function and Memory API (FFM API), a part of the JVM's forthcoming features. The FFM API is particularly notable for its robust mechanisms in managing the lifecycle of foreign resources, ensuring proper deallocation of memory and preventing memory leaks. Additionally, it offers structured foreign memory access, allowing applications to interact seamlessly with complex data structures in foreign memory. These capabilities enhance the interoperability of Java code with native libraries, aligning with the industry consensus on the need for more efficient and secure memory management strategies. The future, as sketched out in this book, invites developers to embrace adaptation and growth, leveraging the full spectrum of capabilities offered by these advanced accelerators.

In conclusion, the contribution of Dr. Juan Fumero and his team is not just a leap in technological advancement; it is a beacon guiding the future of computing. Their work is a compelling invitation to developers and researchers alike to explore and exploit the untapped potential of heterogeneous hardware. As we step into this new era, their research stands as a cornerstone in the ever-expanding edifice of computer science, inspiring and shaping the path forward. "Happy coding," indeed, as we embark on this exciting journey of discovery and innovation.

Monica Beckwith
Java Champion, Author of JVM Performance Engineering—Inside OpenJDK and the HotSpot Java Virtual Machine

Foreword by Gary Frost

I have been an enthusiastic supporter of Juan, Athanasios and Christos' work at Manchester University since I first became aware of their TornadoVM project in 2019. Their project goals aligned very closely with my own attempts at democratizing access to heterogeneous compute when I worked at AMD. Independently, the TornadoVM team and I concluded that, by offering a compelling Java solution, heterogeneous compute performance could be made available to millions of developers rather than a relative handful of OpenCL and CUDA developers.

This book introduces the reader to heterogeneous programming and goes on to discuss the opportunities and unique challenges that arise from interfacing existing heterogeneous runtimes with modern managed runtimes such as the Java Virtual Machine. It also demonstrates concrete implementations of various data parallel algorithms using TornadoVM's Java-friendly programming model.

In my mind TornadoVM is the current state of the art for expressing the code required to execute data parallel workloads in Java.

Gary Frost
Java Platform Group Architect, Oracle

Foreword by Ruyman Reyes Castro

As CTO of Codeplay Software, I have been working with many semiconductor companies and software developers over many years trying to solve the problem of programmability of complex architectures. Many of those customers and users have reached out to me asking what they need to get high languages like Java accelerated by their chip, or what software stack is needed to run PyTorch. This leads to large and complex explanations as to why this is not a simple problem to solve, and why they need to understand a "managed runtime system", virtual machines and garbage collection. Many times I have mentioned or forwarded the work in TornadoVM and others by authors of this book, both as an illustration of how they can solve their problem and also as a good reference to what the problems they need to consider are. This book is a good overview of managed runtime systems that I can use as a point of reference for concepts and examples that can help discussions with developers and customers.

Ruyman Reyes Castro
CTO Codeplay Software

Foreword by Polychronis Xekalakis

While the demand for faster systems increases at a steady rate, the slowdown of Moore's law and Dennard's scaling means that CPU systems cannot easily keep up. As a result, accelerated computing has emerged as a means to provide substantial performance improvements with every new generation. These systems still rely on CPUs, but tightly couple them with accelerators that can offload some part of the computation and execute it much faster than a CPU would be able to. The value of such systems can be better appreciated when looking at cases where they have been deployed. A prime example is that of Deep Learning. The advances in the field were only possible due to the performance provided by these systems being tens of thousands of times faster than what CPU only solutions could be, which in turn allowed for significantly bigger and more complex neural networks.

This book provides a brief introduction of Heterogeneous Hardware such as the one used for accelerated computing. The focus of the book is on the architecture from a programmer's and system software's point of view. Based on real examples of how these systems can be programmed, it provides insights in the considerations that go into play in doing so. More specifically, topics such as software productivity, maintainability and overall performance are being discussed in a clear and concise manner. The authors show that a Managed Runtime system can provide a cleaner interface to the programmer, relieving them from the internals of languages such as CUDA and OpenCL that deal with programming the accelerator and moving data to and from it, and letting them focus on their productivity.

The "Programming Heterogeneous Hardware via Managed Runtime Systems" book is an excellent reference for anyone interested in the field, providing hands-on examples and references for how to think about and program heterogeneous hardware systems.

Dr. Polychronis Xekalakis
Senior Distinguished Engineer, Nvidia Corporation

Acknowledgments

In a rapidly evolving technological landscape, there is an increasingly critical need for a book addressing the gap between managed runtime systems and modern hardware, bridging the understanding gap and empowering developers to optimize performance in an era where efficient utilization of hardware capabilities is crucial. Embarking on the journey of writing this technical book has been a profound and rewarding experience, one that demanded persistent dedication and commitment. The culmination of countless hours of experimentation, analysis, and collaboration with brilliant colleagues has shaped the insights presented in these chapters. I extend my deepest gratitude to my family, especially to my wife, Anna, and to my colleagues whose intellectual contributions have been integral to the book's substance. This work stands as a testament to the remarkable synergy of our collaborative efforts over the past decade, and I am profoundly thankful for the privilege of sharing this collective achievement with you all.

Juan

Writing a book is not a solitary endeavor; it takes the support and encouragement of many wonderful individuals. First and foremost, I would like to express my sincere gratitude to my parents, whose unwavering support and understanding made it possible for me to embark on this writing journey. I extend my heartfelt thanks to my sister and my brother-in-law as well as my nephew and niece for empowering me with their love and our invaluable play time. Your love and belief in me fueled my determination.

Athanasios

To my wife Fiona and my son Panagiotis for all the love, support, and encouragement they give me throughout my life. This book would not be possible without you.

Christos

Contents

Chapter 1
Introduction

1.1 Emergence of Heterogeneous Systems

The computational demands have been increasing especially during the last two decades with the introduction of social media, advanced data analytics, and Artificial Intelligence/Machine Learning applications [13]. Historically, these demands were being fulfilled by newer generations of hardware that were delivering significant performance increases generation-over-generation. As shown in Fig. 1.1, the transistor count and hence Central Processing Unit (CPU) performance has been increasing steadily over the last three decades.

However, as can be seen in Fig. 1.1, the transistor count—and consequently the performance deltas—generation-over-generation have been decreasing mainly due to the slowdown of Moore's law [19] and Dennard scaling [20]. To address the ongoing performance needs, both industry and academia have been investing in heterogeneous hardware systems. Instead of pushing the limited CPU performance boundaries to satisfy all workloads, investments have been made to create dedicated hardware accelerators that are suitable for specific workloads. In the case of heterogeneous systems, instead of having a single CPU trying to execute all workloads, several diverse hardware units or devices are present which execute different parts of applications.

Heterogeneous systems have become pervasive and can be found in a wide range of devices from smartphones to High Performance Computers (HPC). A combination of CPUs, Graphics Processing Units (GPUs), Tensor Processing Units (TPUs), Field Programmable Gate Arrays (FPGAs) and other types of accelerators can be found in today's systems either as discrete hardware devices or embedded in System-on-Chips (SoCs) with the main CPU.

J. Fumero et al., *Programming Heterogeneous Hardware via Managed Runtime Systems*, SpringerBriefs in Computer Science, https://doi.org/10.1007/978-3-031-49559-5_1

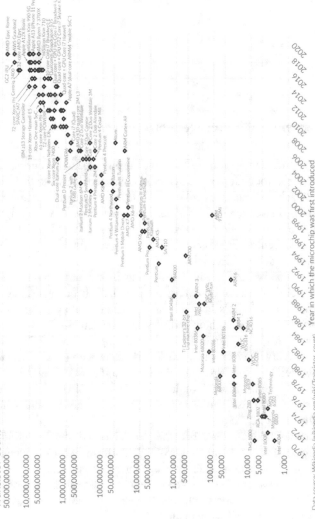

Fig. 1.1 Transistor counts in CPUs over the years [18]

Designing different types of hardware accelerators for different parts of an application cannot only result in performance benefits but also in energy savings, since designing dedicated hardware for dedicated tasks or workloads can lead to more optimal designs [21].

In essence, the key success factors of heterogeneous systems lie in the following requirements:

- **Workload suitability:** *Is my workload suitable for hardware acceleration? If yes, which type of accelerator is ideal?*
- **Programmability:** *How can we efficiently program those accelerators? Are the various heterogeneous programming models compatible with my application?*

This book discusses the advances in heterogeneous systems and how these advances address the aforementioned key success factors, specifically, in the area of managed programming languages. In particular, it presents how managed runtime environments (MREs) can benefit from heterogeneous execution, what challenges they pose, and how current implementations address those challenges.

The rest of this chapter is organized as follows: Sect. 1.2 gives an overview to heterogeneous managed runtime environments, while Sect. 1.3 introduces the key challenges when trying to bring together heterogeneous hardware acceleration and high-level managed programming languages. Finally, Sect. 1.4 presents the structure of this book.

1.2   Introduction to Heterogeneous Managed Runtime Environments

The term *heterogeneous managed runtime environment* [22] refers to the augmentation of current MREs to support execution on heterogeneous hardware accelerators. Traditional MREs such as the Java Virtual Machine (JVM) [24], Microsoft's CLR [25], Python's VM [26] and others, have been initially designed and implemented to support only CPUs by adhering to the *write-once-run-everywhere* paradigm.

According to this paradigm, programs written in high-level programming languages such as Java, .NET, or Python can be executed unmodified across different CPUs that support different Instruction Set Architectures (ISAs) (e.g., x86 [27], ARM [28]). To enable this functionality, MREs that support the execution of those high level programming languages, undertake the task of creating machine code compatible with the specific underlying architecture. Hence, it is the responsibility of the engineers and system designers of MREs to add support for different ISAs to extend the reach of programming languages across different architectures.

Naturally, the constant evolution of hardware and the introduction of heterogeneous hardware accelerators ignited the transition of traditional MREs to heterogeneous MREs which aim to incorporate heterogeneous hardware accelerators, such as GPUs, FPGAs, and TPUs, into their execution capabilities. During the last decade, both industry and academia have contributed ideas and system designs for heterogeneous MREs, aiming to address the particular challenges that MREs pose to heterogeneous hardware acceleration. Systems, such as Apache TVM [29], Keras [30], PyTorch [45], Tensorflow [46], Aparapi [48], Numba [79], TornadoVM [47], IBM J9 [49], are just a handful of examples of the plethora of systems that have been recently introduced.

The existing systems differ in various degrees, such as:

- **Maturity:** While some systems are well established and widely used in production, some others are in a research stage at various Technology Readiness Levels (TRL).
- **Domain:** The application domains targeted by the various systems might differ. While some systems focus on a specific area, such as AI or Machine Learning, some others might be more general purpose.
- **Capabilities:** The capabilities of various systems may differ significantly both in terms of achieved performance and in terms of the number and types of hardware accelerators they can target.
- **Compatibility:** The compatibility of the existing systems with high-level programming languages can differ significantly. In addition, even between systems that target the same programming languages, the way that heterogeneous hardware acceleration is achieved may differ dramatically.

Regardless of the number of differences or capabilities that existing systems have, the challenges that MREs have with respect to heterogeneous hardware acceleration are common. The next section introduces those challenges which will be further elaborated in Chap. 4.

1.3   Challenges in Heterogeneous Managed Runtime Environments

The advent of heterogeneous hardware accelerators resulted in existing programming languages to start embracing them in various ways. Enabling a programming language to harness diverse hardware units can involve different types of integrations with different types of capabilities. For example, a language may be able to expose a GPU to developers via an external library or it can directly emit GPU code at the assembly level via augmentation of its compiler. While both approaches are valid and can indeed enable access to accelerators, they differ significantly in terms of programmability, device coverage, code size, etc. Chapters 3 and 5, describe in detail the current approaches that developers can use in order to utilize heterogeneous hardware.

Each programming language, and its associated runtime(s), has its own challenges while trying to expand its capability in utilizing new hardware devices; especially if these diverse hardware accelerators are constantly evolving in terms of capabilities and workload suitability. Despite all language-dependent differences, there is a number of common challenges across groups of languages that share similar characteristics.

In this book, we focus on managed programming languages; that is, programming languages that typically require the presence of an MRE to execute on. Despite the MREs are different across languages and implementations, they typically share common characteristics, such as code interpretation, Just-In-Time (JIT) compilation, automatic memory management and others. Consequently, those common characteristics pose common challenges when trying to integrate heterogeneous hardware accelerators:

- **Code generation:** *How is the code which will run on the hardware accelerator generated?*
- **Runtime support:** *What kind of runtime support is required for hardware accelerators?*
- **Memory management:** *How is memory managed between the MRE which runs on the CPU and the hardware accelerator?*

The aforementioned challenges are further elaborated in Chap. 4, while Chap. 5 details how current implementations address those challenges.

1.4 Structure

The primary objective of this book is to provide information related to how managed runtime environments are currently being broadened in order to accommodate heterogeneous hardware execution. To better understand how these new hardware devices operate compared to traditional CPUs, how they are programmed, and what challenges they pose to traditional MREs, we provide background information as follows:

- Chapter 2 introduces heterogeneous hardware by providing a detailed explanation on how they operate and how they differ compared to traditional CPUs. Since it is out of scope of this book to present in detail all the different hardware accelerators that exist in the market, we focus the discussion on the most ubiquitous one; General Purpose Graphics Processing Units (GPGPUs). GPUs are pervasive across a plethora of application domains ranging from graphics processing to training of AI and Machine Learning models.
- Chapter 3 discusses current heterogeneous programming models, their characteristics, and how they are being currently used by developers.
- Chapter 4 introduces the internals of MREs, their key components, and how these components pose challenges to heterogeneous execution.

After having introduced the necessary background information on heterogeneous hardware, heterogeneous programming models, and managed runtime environments, the book transitions to Chap. 5 where the current solutions on programming heterogeneous MREs are described. The discussion related to adding heterogeneous hardware support in MREs, evolves around the challenges introduced in Chap. 4; and for each current existing solution the advantages and disadvantages associated with it are discussed. Finally, Chap. 6 concludes this book.

Please note, that research and development on heterogeneous MREs is evolving at a rapid phase and future solutions may not be covered in this book. In addition, a number of examples and exercises are provided online [14–17], giving an opportunity to the reader to practice the theoretical concepts introduced throughout.

Chapter 2
Heterogeneous Hardware

2.1 Introduction to Heterogeneous Computing

The goal of parallel and heterogeneous programming is to run applications more efficiently, either by running faster or by reducing power consumption. Thus, in a sense, parallel programming can be seen as an optimization problem. Hence, when we try to optimize applications, we need to comprehend not only the parallel programming model we are targeting but also the computing architecture that the applications will be deployed on. Depending on the parallel programming model and parallel programming framework, the need to fully understand how hardware executes parallel programs by developers is essential.

One can argue that if we program with high-level parallel programming models, there is actually little or no need to understand the low level architectural details. However, as a system and performance software engineer, it is essential to understand how and why things do not execute nominally, and why specific compilers and runtime systems execute parallel applications the way they do. The goal in this chapter is to provide to readers a good foundation of the hardware differences between CPU and specialized hardware by first giving a very high-level overview of how modern CPUs work, and afterwards explaining GPUs as a hardware accelerator. Note that our goal with this overview is not to provide a full coverage of all CPU components but rather to highlight the main architecture decisions of the development of modern CPUs, and contrast the CPU execution model with the new hardware accelerators. Consequently, we will delve deeper into GPU architectures.

We focus on GPUs because, nowadays, those are the most pervasive accelerators commonly found across compute segments ranging from smartphones, desktop computers, and cloud service providers. In addition, GPUs are widely used for a plethora of diverse workloads spanning for Machine Learning, Deep Learning, AI, and Big Data Analytics to Fintech. In the context of GPUs, we will explain two GPU

J. Fumero et al., *Programming Heterogeneous Hardware via Managed Runtime Systems*, SpringerBriefs in Computer Science, https://doi.org/10.1007/978-3-031-49559-5_2

microarchitectures, NVIDIA Ada GPUs [102], and Intel ARC Alchemist discrete GPUs [11]. Finally, we showcase how code is executed on GPU architectures and this execution differs from CPU execution. If you are familiar with heterogeneous programming and the architectural differences between GPUs and GPUs, we still recommend reading this chapter, since we will set up the terminology and concepts for the rest of this book.

2.2   How do Current CPUs Work?

To understand the differences between CPUs and GPUs, and how GPUs execute instructions, we will first take a brief look at how CPUs work. The goal of this section is just to highlight the main components of the CPU, and explain how instructions and data flow in the processors that are part of the execution of user applications. This section does not cover the full and rich literature on CPU computer architecture, but rather discusses the important information that we can use to contrast CPU and GPU architectures.

As the name implies, a CPU is the central processing component of a computer. CPUs execute machine instructions from computer programs, and it is sometimes referred as the "brain" of the whole computer system, since they are the primary units for executing user and system (OS) instructions. Essentially, CPUs perform a series of operations in a synchronized manner to execute code.

Figure 2.1 shows a high-level representation of how CPUs are connected to the rest of the computing system such as the main memory and the I/O devices. As we will discuss, modern CPUs are composed of CPU-cores. Each core can process

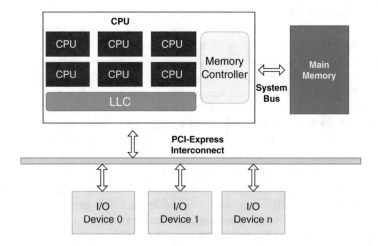

Fig. 2.1 High-level representation of how CPUs interconnect with the rest of the system memory and peripherals

instructions concurrently with the other CPU cores. CPU cores also implement different levels of cache memory (a fast memory to store frequently accessed data and instructions). Figure 2.1 shows what is called the Last Level Cache (LLC), which, for many CPUs, correspond to the L3 cache for storing data. All peripherals are connected to a bus (commonly the PCIe).

Instructions are executed in a stage pipeline. A common pipeline of operations that CPUs perform are as follows:

- **Fetch**: The CPU fetches instructions from memory. The program counter (PC) keeps track of the memory address of the next instruction to be executed.
- **Decode**: The fetched instruction is then decoded to determine what operation needs to be performed. This involves breaking down the instruction into its opcode (the operation code) and operands (the data on which the operation is to be performed).
- **Execute**: The CPU performs the operation indicated by the opcode on the specified operands. This may involve arithmetic or logic operations, data transfers, or control operations.
- **Write-back**: The result of the operation is written back to a register or memory location, depending on the type of the operation.

This process is known as the Fetch-Decode-Execute cycle and is repeated for every instruction in the program. Figure 2.2 shows a common representation of this Fetch-Decode-Execute cycle in CPU pipelines. On the right-hand side, some instructions are shown. These are assembly instructions that load floating point numbers from memory, perform an addition and store the result in a new array in memory. The CPU will load each of these instructions from the main memory into the CPU instruction cache (named L1-I cache). Then, it will decode the instructions to obtain the operations that the CPU needs to perform (e.g., an addition), and separate the data from the rest of the instruction bytes. Once the instruction has been decoded, it is then executed using the internal functional units of the CPU. Modern CPUs contain many types of functional units: for example to perform integer arithmetic, floating point arithmetic, etc. Once the instruction has been executed, the CPU stores the final result into the internal registers.

Although it appears that this execution model executes instructions in order one by one, in reality, CPU instruction pipelines are more sophisticated, and therefore, more complicated. Keep in mind that the goal of the CPU is to execute a single

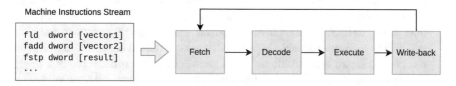

Fig. 2.2 Common pipeline of operations implemented on CPU to obtain instructions from memory, decode the instructions, and execute them

instruction as fast as possible, in other words, execute instructions with very low latency. To do so, modern CPUs implement out-of-order CPUs with superscalar execution with multiple memory cache levels, and sophisticated branch predictors to minimize latency and improve the overall performance.

The pipelining technique divides the CPU's execution into stages, as we saw in Fig. 2.2, allowing multiple instructions to be processed concurrently. This overlaps instruction execution and, therefore, it increases throughput. The way it works is that, while one instruction is being executed (in the execution stage), the next instruction could be in the decode stage and the next instruction could be in the prefetch stage.

Furthermore, modern CPUs may execute instructions out of order. This means that instructions that do not depend on the results of previous instructions can be executed ahead of others; further improving performance. This is done in hardware, but compilers also play an important role in reordering the instructions.

CPUs also make use of different levels of memory caches (small units of fast memory) that store frequently used data and instructions. This reduces the time that is required to access data from slower memories, such as DRAM.

Lastly, CPUs also implement branch predictors with the goal of predicting, in advance, if a specific branch of the instruction stream will be taken or not taken. This has a lot of influence in performance, because in the case of misprediction, the CPU needs to flush all instructions from the stream that are in the middle of the execution of the CPU pipeline. Thus, if a branch can be predicted ahead of time (before the instruction is in the prefect stage), it can reduce latency.

Multi-Core CPUs

Modern CPUs contain multiple processing units (cores) on a single chip. Each core can operate independently, and it has its own instruction pipeline, making it capable of performing parallel computation. Multi-core CPUs were created to address several challenges as described below:

- **Performance scaling**: As mentioned in the introduction, CPU performance was initially improved by increasing the frequency (clock speed) of a single-core processor. However, this approach imposes physical and thermal limitations as clock speed reached their maximum limits. Thus, multi-core processors were introduced as a way to continue improving performance without increasing the frequency. By adding more cores per single chip, CPUs can process independent instructions in parallel, enhancing the overall performance of the applications.
- **Power efficiency:** Similarly to performance frequency scaling, CPUs also consumed more and more power and generated more heat. Multi-core CPUs offer a way to improve computational power while keeping power consumption and heat to more manageable levels. This can be achieved because the workload can be distributed across different CPU cores, and each core can run at a lower frequency and voltages, resulting in a more balanced system between achieving higher performance and required energy.
- **Demand for more computing power:** Many modern applications such as Graphics Rendering, Video Processing, Data Analytics, etc., require more

demanding CPUs to process these heavily computing programs. Multi-core CPUs enable more computing, as different cores can be used for different tasks while operating simultaneously.

Multi-core CPUs have evolved to include more parallel processing, lower latency by increasing cache sizes, and improved hardware to perform branch prediction. Let's now explore the different techniques that CPUs employ for performing parallel computation:

Exploiting Parallelism on Multi-Core CPUs

There is a number of ways in which multi-core CPUs exploit parallelism:

1. **Instruction Level Parallelism (ILP):** Just as a single-core CPUs, multi-core CPUs can exploit ILP by processing multiple instructions concurrently within the same instruction pipeline. One part of the instruction can be in the execution stage, while processing the fetch and decode for the next two instructions. In addition, ILP occurs per CPU-core. Thus, each CPU offers ILP from the original instruction stream.

2. **Data Parallelism (vector instructions):** Modern multi-core CPUs also offer Single Instruction, Multiple Data (SIMD) instructions, as a way to compute a function for a range of elements in a single CPU instruction. This technique allows parallel applications such as video processing and multimedia to operate faster.

3. **Hyper-threading (HT) within the CPU-core:** This is a common technique to enhance the performance of a single core of a CPU. The idea is that the hardware can simulate the presence of a new core (a logical core) to increase the utilization of the CPU resources, such as functional units. Since modern CPUs implement complex hardware pipelines for executing the stream of instructions, it might happen that not all functional units are utilized within a single stage of the pipeline. In this situations, HT can increase performance by interleaving instructions that do not share the same resources. Note that, if two HT threads share the same resources, performance can potentially degrade. Thus, there is a trade-off between having more threads (which potentially execute independent instructions), and application types.

4. **HT and multi-core:** All the aforementioned techniques can be combined for each CPU core, giving the CPU with plenty of resources for performing parallel computations.

Figure 2.3 shows the floor plan of an Intel Raptor Lake processor i9-13900K. This is the latest processor from Intel at the time of writing this book and it shows the distribution of the die area, dedicated to each CPU component. This CPU has eight performance cores (P-cores) and twelve efficiency cores (E-cores). Each core has its own L1 and L2 cache. As we can see, most of the die area of the chip is dedicated to control and cache.

Based on the current high performance CPUs available on the market, someone may wonder why CPUs are not enough to cover our computational needs. Why do we need additional specialized coprocessors in our systems? CPUs are optimized

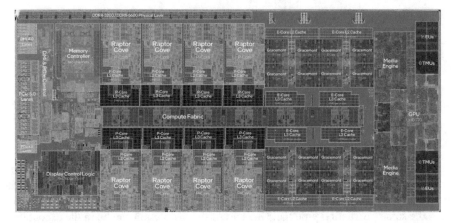

Fig. 2.3 Floor plan of the Intel Raptor Lake i9-13900K (13th generation of the Intel core processors). Image taken from Wikipedia [96]

to run low-latency applications. However, there is an increasing demand for more parallel processing to compute domain specific applications more efficiently. For example, processing applications for AI workloads. As we will see in the next section, there is new hardware optimized for domain specific applications than can process programs in a more efficient way.

2.3   What Is a GPU and How does it Work?

Graphics Processing Units (GPUs) are specialized coprocessors for rendering graphics in real-time; with a high focus on video games. While the original focus of GPUs was computing graphics, today's GPUs are also programmable and are able to execute general-purpose applications (known as GPGPUs—General Purpose GPU). Apart from computing graphics (usually through APIs such as DirectX [2], OpenGL [3], and Vulkan [4]), GPUs can be used to increase the performance of domain specific and general purpose applications such as Deep Learning, Machine Learning, Physics/Math Simulations, Computer Vision, and Big Data processing. Note that GPU programming models are Turing Complete [1]. This means that, given enough time and enough memory, any computation can be performed. GPUs are also relatively affordable in comparison with an equivalent high-performance CPU computing system. For these reasons, many developers are incorporating GPUs in their execution workflow as a way to process workloads more efficiently by increasing performance and saving energy consumption of the whole system.

Very Brief History of GPUs
GPUs are evolved coprocessors from VGA (Video Graphics Array) controllers [6]. These controllers contained a display generator and a memory controller con-

nected to a DRAM. During the 1990s, VGA controllers were evolving with more specialized functions which included, for example, two-dimensional and three-dimensional functions. Additionally, VGAs started incorporating more complex hardware pipelines to process graphics, such as stages to compute geometry, triangles, and rasterization.

In 1999, the first GPU was released. NVIDIA, with its GeForce 256 coined the term Graphics Processing Unit (GPUs) [5] which incorporated more complex functions for real-time graphics processing. Over the years, not only GPUs got more generic, but also programmable. NVIDIA redesigned some graphic pipeline stages for rendering graphics to make the GPUs more programmable. The new more programmable graphic pipeline was not only useful for graphics, but also for general computation (known as GPGPU).

The history of GPUs has been marked by a rapid pace of innovation, driven by the demands of the gaming, multimedia, and computing industries. Today, GPUs are critical components of many modern computing systems for many software applications, and their role is only expected to grow as new applications for AI and machine-learning continue to emerge [7].

Graphics Pipeline
GPU hardware implements a complex set of graphics functions in the various pipeline stages. Some of these functions are fixed in hardware, thus, are non-programmable, and others are programmable. In general, the shader stages are programmable, and they manipulate as input of vertices to provide colors, and textures.

Graphics shaders are small programs that are used in a GPU pipeline to control how 3D objects and surfaces are rendered in a computer screen. There are several types of shaders in modern GPUs. The most common ones are vertex shaders, which are used to process different vertices of objects in a 3D model; geometry shaders which manipulate vertices further, such as calculating textures; and pixel shaders which compute the final lighting, textures and transparency for each pixel. Each type of shader serves a different purpose and can be used to create a wide variety of visual effects and computational tasks.

Figure 2.4 shows a list of stages in a computer graphics pipeline on modern GPUs. The green blocks show the programmable stages; namely, the vertex, geometry, and pixel shaders. The input program for a vertex shader is typically a set of vertices and their associated attributes, such as position, color and texture coordinates. Then, each vertex data item is processed by the vertex shader and the and geometry shader. After that, the new vertices are passed to the rasterization stage. The function of a rasterizer in a graphics pipeline is to convert the geometric primitives generated by the previous stages of the pipeline into fragments, which are individual pixels on the screen. After processing the pixels in the pixel shader, they are passed to the raster operations stage. This stage involves a set of operations that can be performed on the fragments generated by the rasterizer stage of the graphics pipeline before the final output is written to a frame buffer. These operations can

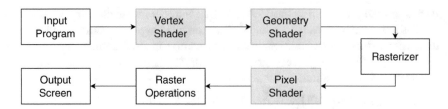

Fig. 2.4 Example of a Graphics Pipeline operation in modern GPUs. The green blocks depict the programmable stages while the white blocks show the fixed functions

be used to modify the attributes of the fragments or to combine them with other fragments to generate the final color value for each pixel.

2.4 How Are GPUs Connected to the System?

Before diving into the GPU architectures, let's have a look at how GPUs are interconnected with the rest of the computing systems in modern setups. There are two main types of GPUs that are used in current computing systems: discrete GPUs (dGPUs) and integrated GPUs (iGPUs).

An integrated GPU is built into the CPU itself and shares the system's main memory, while a discrete GPU is a separate component that has its own dedicated memory. In order for a computer to utilize both types of GPUs, the CPU must have the necessary hardware and software interfaces to communicate with them. Typically, the motherboard of a computer will have slots for discrete GPUs to be installed, and the GPU will connect to the motherboard using a PCI-Express interface.

Figure 2.5 shows two representations of a computing architecture for: a) an integrated GPU system, and b) two discrete GPUs connected to the system. The integrated GPU resides inside the CPU die, and it shares the Last Level Cache (LLC) with the CPU. The main memory is connected through a system bus to the CPUs (right-hand side of Fig. 2.5). Discrete GPUs, on the other hand, have their own memory, and they are connected to the system via PCI-e. Thus, usually, memory buffers need to be transferred from the CPU's main memory to the GPU's memory for maximizing throughput on the GPU. We will discuss more details about the programming model in the next chapter.

GPUs can be interconnected to each other via a proprietary connector. For example, NVIDIA employs the NVLINK [12] connector interface. NVLINK is a high-bandwidth, low-latency interface that enables fast data transfers between GPUs, allowing them to work together as a unified system. It provides a faster and more efficient way for GPUs to communicate with each other and share data, compared to other interconnect technologies such as PCI-e. To put this in perspective, PCI-e version 5 supports data transfers of up to 63 GB/s, while the

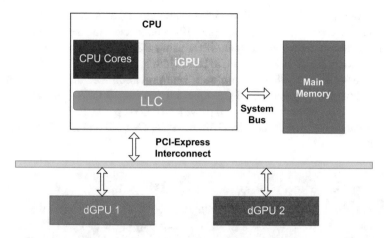

Fig. 2.5 High-Level representation of a CPU architecture and two GPU configurations: an integrated GPU (iGPU) and two discrete GPUs (dGPUs) that are connected through PCIe to the computing system

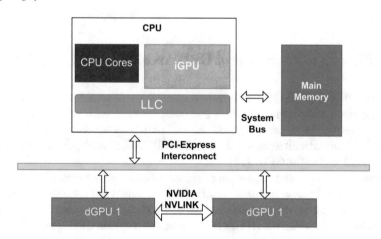

Fig. 2.6 Example of a computing system with multiple discrete GPUs interconnected through an NVIDIA NVLINK connection

NVIDIA NVLINK Gen4 (the latest NVILINK technology at the time of writing this book), is 900 GB/s (14x theoretical faster operation). Note that, in reality, it may be less than 14x due to application constraints.

Figure 2.6 shows an example of a computing system using multiple discrete GPUs interconnected through an NVIDIA NVLINK connector. Note that this type of setup works only when connected to specific models of NVIDIA GPUs (e.g., NVIDIA GP100).

It is important to pay attention to the bandwidth of data transfers between the host and device when having multiple GPUs connected to the same computing system. When connecting multiple GPUs using PCIe, the available bandwidth is shared between the devices. The PCIe bandwidth is typically expressed in terms of the number of lanes available, with each lane providing a certain amount of data transfer capacity. For example, PCIe Gen 3.0 provides 8 GT/s (gigatransfers per second) per lane, while PCIe Gen 4.0 provides 16 GT/s per lane. So, for a PCIe x16 slot, the bandwidth would be 128 GB/s for PCIe Gen 3.0 and 256 GB/s for PCIe Gen 4.0.

When multiple GPUs are connected to the same PCIe root complex, the available bandwidth is divided among the devices. Therefore, if two GPUs are connected in two PCIe x16 slots that end up to the same root complex, each GPU would operate with bandwidth of up to 8 GT/s (PCIe Gen 3.0) or 16 GT/s (PCIe Gen 4.0).

2.5 High-Level Overview of GPU Architectures

Let's deep dive into the GPU architecture itself. We will start describing, at a high level, the main components of GPUs and compare them with a CPU architecture. This will set up the terminology and the main building blocks to understand the recent GPU microarchitectures, such as the NVIDIA Ada micro-architecture [102] and the Intel Alchemist GPUs [11].

Figure 2.7 shows a very high-level schematic of a computing system composed of a multi-core CPU that contains an integrated GPU, and a discrete GPU. Figure 2.7 also shows a high-level representation of how the system memory and hardware accelerators such as discrete GPUs are connected to the main CPU. The CPU access the main memory through the system bus, while discrete GPUs access memory via PCIe.

Let's start by describing the main components on the CPU side. The CPU is composed of multiple cores. Each core has its own set of registers, L1 cache (L1 Data and L1 Instructions cache), and L2 cache. For simplification, we do not show these details in the diagram of Fig. 2.7. Furthermore, cores within the CPU contain a set of functional units to perform operations such as integer and floating point arithmetic and vector operations. The CPU also contains an L3, which is commonly known as the Last Level Cache (LLC). This LLC is shared between all CPU cores and the integrated GPU (iGPU).

The integrated GPU is a specialized hardware for real-time graphics rendering. As such, it usually contains more functional units than cache and memory. The iGPU represented in Fig. 2.7 contains 12 cores for compute as well as two special

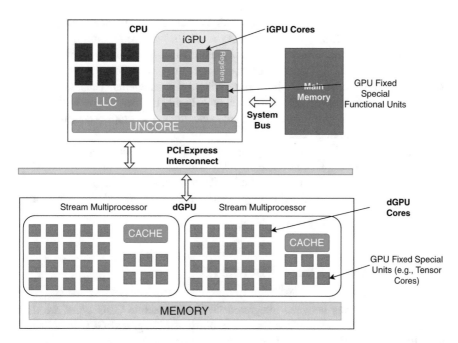

Fig. 2.7 High-level overview of integrated and discrete GPUs architecture and their connection with the main system

functional units. GPUs usually contain lots of simpler cores compared to the CPUs. The computing cores usually perform operations in integer and single-precision floating point arithmetic. For more complex functions, such as double precision or complex math operations, such as square root, GPUs usually provide dedicated functional units that are shared across a set of compute cores. Besides its own computation cores, GPUs provide a large set of registers and smaller caches compared to CPUs.

Discrete GPUs (dGPUs) have many similarities with integrated GPUs. They usually provide a set of streaming multiprocessors (SM). Each SM contains a set of thread schedulers (not shown in Fig. 2.7 for simplification) as well as many compute cores and special functional units (e.g., GPU Tensor Cores for tensor computation, which is a type of computation widely use in Deep Learning). The number of physical cores per SM varies per vendor, type of GPU (consumer vs data center GPUs), and generation of the microarchitecture (e.g., NVIDIA Pascal vs NVIDIA Ada). Figure 2.7 shows two SMs as an example, but modern NVIDIA GPUs usually have 80–150 SMs with 64–128 compute cores per SM.

In addition to compute cores, GPUs contain a large number of register files per SM and a shared cache for all SMs. Furthermore, discrete GPUs contain their own DDR memory that is shared among all SMs in the GPU. This DDR memory usually offers much higher bandwidth compared to CPU memory.

The main reason for higher bandwidth is that GPUs are designed for high throughput computations. We will discuss in Chap. 3 the programming model in detail, but in a nutshell, GPUs perform computation in wavefront, or warps, in which each warp (e.g., a set of 32 threads) computes the same instruction (using exactly the same Program Counter—PC -) for different input data elements. Thus, GPUs need high bandwidth in order to keep functional units highly utilized. As we will see, this is not the only strategy to keep GPUs busy, since they also employ multithreading (further discussed in Sect. 2.7.3).

To put the GPU bandwidth in perspective with the whole computing system, modern GPUs employ GDDR6X technology which offers a theoretical bandwidth of up to 1008 GB/s [102] (e.g, on the NVIDIA RTX 4090 GPU), while modern CPU's memory uses DDR5 technology, which offers a theoretical bandwidth of up to 64GB/s.

2.6   Integrated GPUs vs Discrete GPUs

The main differences between integrated GPU and discrete GPU types are their performance, power consumption, and flexibility. An integrated GPU is built into the CPU itself and shares the system's main memory. They are usually less powerful than discrete GPUs, as they have to share resources with the CPU and other system components. Integrated GPUs are often found in low-end and mid-range computers and are suitable for basic tasks like web browsing, multimedia, office applications and even low-compute demanding video games.

On the other hand, a discrete GPU is a separate component that has its own dedicated memory and processing capabilities. It is typically more powerful than integrated GPUs and can handle more demanding tasks like gaming, video editing, and 3D modeling. Discrete GPUs are usually found in high-end gaming and workstation computers and they are more expensive than integrated GPUs.

In terms of power consumption, integrated GPUs are generally more power-efficient than discrete GPUs. This is because they are built into the CPU and use less power to perform basic graphics tasks. Discrete GPUs, on the other hand, require more power to operate and can generate more heat, which can be a concern for smaller or less well-ventilated computer cases.

Another difference between integrated and discrete GPUs is their flexibility. Integrated GPUs are typically fixed and cannot be upgraded or replaced, as they are part of the CPU chip. Discrete GPUs, on the other hand, can be upgraded or replaced, as they are separate components that can be installed or removed as needed.

In addition, since integrated GPUs use the same memory as the CPU system, they offer a unified view of memory, which can benefit many applications, especially for those GPU applications in which the majority of the time is not spent on the kernel itself but rather in the communications.

2.7 How Are GPUs Programmable?

As mentioned earlier, GPUs implement a hardware pipeline of different stages involved in real-time graphics rendering. Figure 2.4 showed the typical stages in a GPU pipeline, and the programmable stages via shaders hardware units, which manipulate vertices and pixels to process, in real-time, the textures, colors and geometry of input shader programs.

Over time, these programmable units became more powerful and suitable for more general computations. Hence, GPU vendors started grouping shaders into unified processors called Unified Shader Architectures (also called Unified Array Processors).

Unified Shader Architecture is a GPU design concept that allows for a more flexible and efficient use of computational resources. Traditional GPU architectures separated the pixel, geometry, and vertex processing stages into fixed-function units (as we saw in Fig. 2.4), which meant that each unit could only perform a specific type of operation. This approach had limited flexibility and was not well-suited to modern computing tasks which often require more complex and varied processing tasks.

With Unified Shader Architecture, the GPU can dynamically allocate processing resources based on the needs of the specific application, resulting in more efficient use of computational resources. For example, if an application requires more pixel processing power than vertex processing power, the GPU can allocate more resources to the pixel shaders.

Another advantage of Unified Shader Architecture is that it enables more efficient programming of GPU applications. Rather than having to write separate code for the pixel and vertex stages, developers can write a single shader program that can be executed on the unified shader core. The Unified Shader Architecture was first introduced by ATI (now AMD) in their Radeon X1000 series of GPUs in 2005 [8], and it has since become a standard feature in modern GPUs both from AMD and Nvidia.

Figure 2.8 shows a high-level representation of a Unified Shader Processor that contains a vertex shader, geometry shader and pixel shader in the same unit. These architectural components can be programmable using a suitable shader programming language (e.g., Microsoft Direct X, OpenCL, and Vulkan).

With the Unified Shader Architecture, GPUs moved towards to a more flexible and programmable design. Instead of having separate circuits for each stage, a unified set of shaders was introduced. These shaders could be dynamically allocated and utilized for different tasks as needed, such as vertex processing, geometry processing, or pixel processing. This flexibility allowed for more efficient resource utilization and reduced the complexity of the circuits.

By unifying the shaders, GPUs became more programmable and adaptable to different graphics workloads. It simplified the design and reduced the overall hardware complexity by eliminating redundant circuitry. This simplification not only made GPUs more efficient in terms of power consumption and performance

Fig. 2.8 Example of a
Unified Shader Processor on
a GPU hardware pipeline

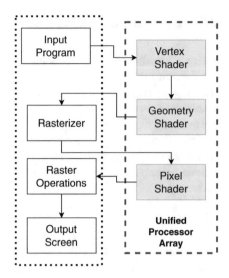

but also paved the way for more advanced graphics techniques and increased
programmability.

2.7.1 Using Shaders for General Purpose Computation

Since GPUs were originally designed to render pixels on the screen as fast
as possible, the hardware was inherently parallel. Each pixel can be computed
independently of any other pixel on the screen. Furthermore, to process all pixels
in real time, GPUs evolved to include high-performance floating point arithmetic,
offering higher bandwidths compared to CPUs. However, to program those GPUs,
applications must be expressed as a rendering algorithm.

As GPU shaders became more programmable, researchers started to study and
investigate if GPUs could be used for more than rendering pixels on the screen and
perform more general computation. For example, to solve linear algebra problems
more efficiently, given higher performance and higher bandwidth compared to the
same application running on the CPU. Thus, trying to compute specific types of
applications on these new devices was really appealing to increase performance by
using idle resources of common computing systems.

One of the first general-purpose programming languages to run on GPUs was
BrookGPU [9], the predecessor of the CUDA programming language that we
have today. BrookGPU was developed by Stanford University's Brook project, and
released in 2004.

The goal of Brook was to provide a high-level programming language and
runtime system that would allow developers to leverage the computational power
of GPUs for a wide range of applications beyond graphics. It aimed to simplify

GPU programming by abstracting away the low-level details of GPU architectures and provide a more intuitive programming model.

Brook introduced a **data-parallel programming model**, where computations are expressed in terms of parallel operations on arrays of data. The language included constructs for array operations such as map, reduce, and scan, which allowed developers to express parallel algorithms in a concise and expressive manner. Brook also provided support for user-defined functions and data structures.

Although the BrookGPU programming language did not gain widespread adoption, it presented and showed the foundations for newer parallel programming models such as CUDA and OpenCL. We will show how GPUs are programmed using CUDA and OpenCL in the next chapter.

GPUs can now be used for application domains such as Deep Learning, Fintech, Math and Physics Simulations and Computer Vision, just to name a few, performing hundreds times faster than the equivalent application running on CPUs.

2.7.2   CPUs Versus GPUs: Can GPUs Replace CPUs?

As we have seen in the previous section, if GPUs can run general-purpose applications, one can wonder if we can run everything on the GPU and totally replace the CPU. In short, GPUs cannot completely replace CPUs. While both GPUs and CPUs are types of processors, they are designed for different purposes and excel at different types of tasks. To understand this better, it is important to highlight the main strengths and differences between these two computing devices.

CPUs are general-purpose processors that handle a wide range of tasks in a computer system. They are optimized for handling tasks that require complex control flow, low-latency requirements, sequential processing, and running a variety of software applications. CPUs typically have a smaller number of cores (usually up to 64 cores) and **focus on executing instructions with high single-threaded performance**.

On the other hand, **GPUs are specialized processors**, that, as we have seen, were originally designed for rendering graphics in computer games and other graphical applications. They have a large number of cores (hundreds to thousands) optimized for parallel processing. GPUs are highly efficient at performing data-parallel applications, making them ideal for tasks that involve massive parallelism, such as 3D graphics rendering, machine learning, and scientific computations.

While GPUs can handle certain computational tasks faster than CPUs, they are not as versatile as CPUs when it comes to general-purpose computing. CPUs are essential for managing system operations, running the operating system, handling hardware interrupts, handling connectivity with other devices, executing non-parallel tasks, and handling tasks that require complex decision-making and branching logic. For example, code with multiple branches (complex control flow) may perform very poorly on GPUs, due to the lack of branch predictor hardware units. On the contrary, modern CPUs contain very sophisticated branch predictors. We will expand on how GPUs handle control flow in the following sections.

In practice, a combination of CPUs and GPUs is often used in many computing systems to take advantage of their respective strengths. CPUs handle general-purpose tasks and coordinate overall system operations, while GPUs accelerate specific computations that can be parallelized. This combination allows for efficient and optimized performance across a wide range of applications.

2.7.3 Overview of the GPU Execution Model

An execution model refers to how the hardware executes code. It defines how instructions are executed, the memory model which describes how memory is organized and how it is managed, and how data is manipulated. The execution model plays an important role in shaping the performance and efficiency of computing systems. Furthermore, it also influences how programs are written and optimized. This section provides a general overview of the execution model that will serve as a fundamental pillar to understand GPU programming models in the next chapter.

The GPU execution model follows the Single Instruction Multiple Thread (SIMT) model, which allows a GPU to execute a large number of threads simultaneously. SIMT is a technique that combines execution on multiple data with multithreading, allowing the execution of applications at high throughput.

SIMT can be sometimes referred to as SIMD (Single Instruction Multiple Data). However, there are some key differences: in a SIMD processor, there is one instruction fetcher and decoder per core, and the actual SIMD operation (an operation on multiple values at the same time) occurs in an execution unit within the core (ALU), having a single vision of memory. In contrast, a SIMT processor usually has the same instruction fetch and decoder for a set of instructions (typically 32, but this really depends on the GPU vendor), and instructions are assigned to different GPU cores that execute the same program counter with different data items. Thus, in a SIMT processor, each core has its own stack pointer that performs operations with different data items.

GPU threads are organized into groups called warps (a set of threads that are executed in a lock-step). This means that a single instruction is broadcast to all threads in a warp, and each thread performs the operation on its own set of data. This approach exploits data-level parallelism, where the same operation is applied to multiple data elements simultaneously.

Each **warp** typically consists of 32 threads on NVIDIA GPUs and 64 threads on AMD GPUs (called wavefront). In a SIMT system, multiple warps can be executed concurrently, with the GPU dynamically scheduling them based on available resources.

Let's now dive into the different parts of the GPU execution model. First, we will show a general overview of a GPU with its stream multiprocessors (SM) and their connection to global memory. Then, we will explain the general architecture of an SM. Finally, we will show the memory hierarchy and how synchronization is performed on GPUs.

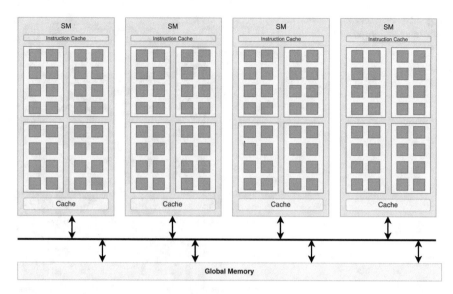

Fig. 2.9 Representation of a Stream Multiprocessor (SM) from the NVIDIA GPU architecture

Figure 2.9 shows a representation of SMs from the NVIDIA GPU architecture. This diagram shows a simplification of the logic within the SM for illustration purposes. However, we will analyze in more detail each of the components in the SM in the following sections.

Each SM contains a set of compute cores (also called CUDA cores) and, in the Ada NVIDIA GPU microarchitecture generation, also includes other types of cores such as tensor cores and ray tracing cores. Each SM has its own bank of register files and a L1 cache. GPUs can contain multiple SMs and the exact number varies per GPU model and GPU architecture generation. Furthermore, each SM has its own local memory (or shared memory) that is visible to all cores within the same SM, and all SMs has the same view of the global memory.

2.7.4 Streaming Multiprocessors

Let's take a closer look at the SM architecture. This is the heart of the GPU architecture and one of the most important components within the GPU system that helps to achieve high throughput and process data-parallel applications efficiently.

Figure 2.10 shows an example of SM architectural components within a GPU. We follow the latest SM architecture from NVIDIA (called SMM), which is an evolution of the original SM. Note that, although there are architectural differences between the original SM and the SMM, the main concepts remain the same. Thus, we continue naming the SMM as SM, however, keep in mind that we refer to the SM

Fig. 2.10 Example of a
streaming multiprocessor
core

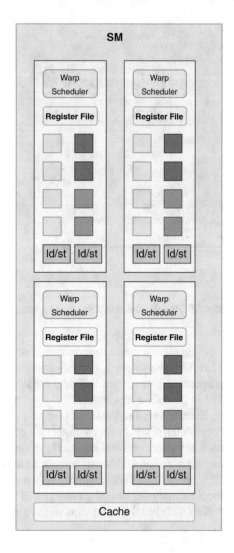

from the NVIDIA GPU Maxwell microarchitecture, and more recently, the NVIDIA
Ada microarchitecture [102].

As we can see in Fig. 2.10, each SM is divided into four partitions. Each partition
has its own warp scheduler. Recall that a warp is a set of 32 threads that run the same
Program Counter (PC) that are executed in parallel with the capability of addressing
different data items. The warp scheduler might also contain a cache of instructions
ready to be executed.

Furthermore, each partition of the SM contains a large register file (usually more
than 10k registers of 32 bits) and a set of Arithmetic Logic Units (ALUs). There
are usually different types of ALUs specialized for different instruction types (e.g.,
ALUs for 32-bit integer arithmetic, floating point 32-bit arithmetic, tensor cores,

and ray tracing cores). Finally, each SM can contain several load/store units that can access local caches and global memory.

An important consideration is the concept of the core. While vendors such as NVIDIA name CUDA core an ALU that performs computation in, for example, 32 bits floating point operation, others consider this core as a functional unit within a core. Each SM can be seen as a core, and all functional units within the SM can be seen as scalar and vector processing units. For reference, an NVIDIA Ada GPU (e.g., RTX 4090) contains 128 SMs, and each SM contains 128 CUDA cores.

2.7.5 Thread Hierarchy and SIMT Execution

Let's take deep dive into how threads are distributed in a SIMT architecture like a GPU. The thread hierarchy of GPUs is a key aspect of the execution model and plays a crucial role in organizing and coordinating the parallel execution of computational tasks. The thread hierarchy consists of three levels: threads, blocks, and grids.

Note that, for this section, we are borrowing the terms from the NVIDIA CUDA terminology. However, there is a one-to-one mapping between the NVIDIA CUDA and other parallel programming models such as OpenCL and oneAPI. For example, the term thread is known as a work-item in OpenCL, while the block is known as a work-group and grid is known as an ND-range.

The gpu thread is the smallest unit of work in the thread hierarchy. It represents an individual execution context and operates on a specific portion of the data. GPU threads are represented in one, two, and three dimensions, allowing programmers to index different ways to access and manipulate data much easier. Threads are organized into blocks.

A set of threads forms a block, in which the number of threads can vary from a few to thousands, depending on the GPU architecture and programming choices. All threads within a block can synchronize with each other and share data using shared memory. We will discuss the memory hierarchy in the next section. Blocks are also organized into a 3D space (1D, 2D, and 3D block of threads). We will discuss more in detail in Chap. 3 when we explain the programming models for GPUs.

The grid is the highest level of the thread hierarchy. It represents the entire set of threads launched by the CPU for execution on the GPU. A grid is defined by the number of blocks in each dimension (1D, 2D and 3D). The size of the grid determines the total number of threads that will be executed.

By organizing threads into grids, blocks, and threads, the GPU execution model enables efficient parallel execution, facilitates data sharing and communication within a block, and maximizes GPU utilization. This hierarchical structure provides programmers with fine-grained control over parallelism and allows for the acceleration of complex computations on GPUs.

Figure 2.11 shows a representation of the different elements of the thread hierarchy on GPUs. At the top level, it is the thread, which is a minimal execution unit. Threads are organized into warps (blocks of threads that are executed together

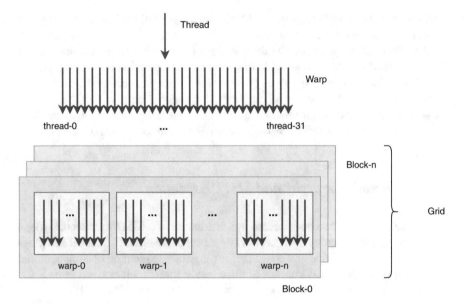

Fig. 2.11 Thread hierarchy of GPUs

in a lock-step manner). Warps, in turn, are organized into blocks. The number of threads per block depends on the input application and resources available on the GPU. Finally, a block of threads is organized into grids.

The thread hierarchy allows for efficient scheduling and coordination of computations following the SIMT execution model. As follows, we explain the steps of this execution model and its coordination with the thread hierarchy of the GPUs.

1. **The CPU (host) launches a grid of threads** by specifying the number of blocks in each dimension and the number of threads per block. For example, the host launches a grid of threads composed of 10 blocks of threads with 256 threads per block. Note that the number of threads and blocks varies per application and input size.
2. Thread management is fully automatic and it is part of the GPU execution. **The GPU scheduler assigns blocks of threads to SMs**. Note that all threads that belong to the same block are assigned to the same SM. This is because, as we will explain in the memory hierarchy, threads within the same block can share memory, while threads assigned to different SMs cannot share memory (use of shared memory only within the SM).
3. **The block of threads within the SM is, in turn, partitioned into warps**. The number of threads per warp may vary depending on the vendor and the architecture generation. The usual number is 32 threads for NVIDIA GPUs and 64 threads for AMD GPUs (called wavefronts). Each SM maintains a queue with wraps that are ready to execute. The SM then assigns a warp to be executed in parallel using the functional units and hardware resources of the SM. All threads

within an SM execute the same instruction in a lock step. This design simplifies the control logic of the chip (for instance, fetch and decode units are shared across a set of threads), and it allows GPUs to integrate more functional units (compute units) and less control logic.

4. **Fast context switching** is possible within SMs. If a warp needs to wait for a data dependency before executing, then the SM can reschedule the whole warp and assign a new warp from the ready list of the scheduler to physical units. This design allows GPUs to operate at high throughput by hiding latencies due to data dependencies or memory operations (e.g., loads or stores from/to the GPU's global memory).

2.7.6   Memory Hierarchy

The SIMT model also supports a memory hierarchy with different levels of memory available on the GPU. Threads can access registers, private memory, shared memory, and global memory.

Registers and private memory are private to each thread and offer the fastest access, but they have limited capacity. Shared memory (or local memory as in the OpenCL terminology) is shared among threads within a block (a collection of warps), allowing for data sharing and inter-thread communication. Global memory is accessible to all threads in the grid (all blocks of threads) and provides the largest capacity at the cost of higher latency.

Figure 2.12 represents the different levels of the memory hierarchy in relation to the thread-level representation. Note that, if data must be shared, it is only possible through two memory entities: (a) shared memory, or (b) global memory. Shared memory offers lower latency compared to global memory but it is limited in three ways:

1. Shared memory has limited capacity. Each GPU generation and GPU architecture provide a different amount of shared memory.
2. Shared memory can be accessed from threads that belong to the same block.
3. Loads and stores into shared memory are not coherent. Thus, to guarantee memory coherency, it is necessary to add barriers or synchronization primitives, as we will discuss in the next subsection.

Finally, the global memory is accessible by all threads within the execution grid. Although the GPU's global memory is the slowest of the hierarchy in terms of latency, it offers very high bandwidth compared to the CPU's main memory. The technology implemented on GPUs is usually HBM (High Bandwidth Memory), such as HBM 3 from the NVIDIA Hopper architecture, which integrates DRAM memory into the GPU package offering up to 3 TB/s of memory bandwidth.

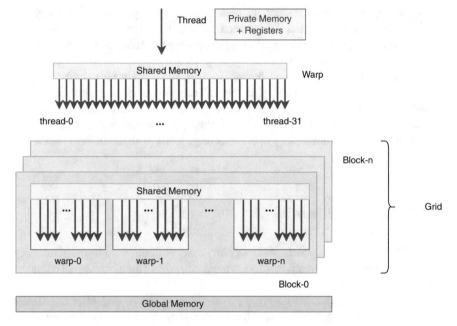

Fig. 2.12 Memory hierarchy of common GPUs for computing

2.7.7 Synchronization

Similarly to the memory and thread hierarchy, synchronization on GPUs can occur at different levels. Let's dive in and discuss the different levels from the most generic synchronization primitives to the smallest unit.

When a GPU kernel is launched, there is an implicit synchronization point. Kernels can be launched asynchronously from the host (main CPU), but the whole function is executed in a block. If a GPU kernel is launched synchronously (the host is blocked until the GPU function is finished), then the CPU thread that launched the kernel is also blocked.

Barriers can be performed at the thread-block level. This means that GPU threads that belong to the same thread block wait for each other if a barrier is encountered. Barriers cannot be performed between threads that belong to different thread blocks.

One thing to consider when programming GPUs is that shared memory on GPUs is not coherent. This means that, in order to enable shared memory, programmers must explicitly add synchronization points (or barriers). However, barriers are only applied per thread block within the same SM. Thus, if memory must be shared across threads, it is important to notice that synchronization points are only guaranteed within threads of the same thread block.

2.7.8   Control Flow Divergence

GPU hardware is extremely efficient at exploiting data parallelism through the SIMT execution model. However, what happens when there is thread divergence? GPU threads are never executed in isolation. Remember that GPUs execute instructions in lockstep via a warp (or wavefront) of threads (e.g., a block of 32 consecutive threads).

When there is control flow divergence, ideally, all GPU threads take the same branch of the control flow (e.g., the same branch in an if-condition). However, this may not be always the case. The GPU hardware maintains a SIMT mask to indicate if a branch is predicated or not. If there is control flow divergence, the GPU usually takes both branches of the control flow divergence, and it uses a mask register to indicate which branches are active and which branches are idle (or non-active). In the worst-case scenario, all threads within a warp take different execution paths. This means that, in the presence of control flow divergence within the GPU kernel execution, the GPU serializes the execution.

This is a trade-off. GPUs provide more functional units to support more threads running concurrently on the accelerator, at the cost of simplifying control logic. Note that, through the mask register and the use of predicated branches, GPUs provide the right execution, at the cost of performance. Thus, from the programmers' perspective, this is fully transparent. However, for performance engineering, this is definitely something to keep in mind.

If possible, it is recommended that programmers minimize control flow, and/or structure the code and data in such a way that minimizes control flow divergence. However, this might not be always possible, and control flow divergence can have a significant negative impact on performance, especially when running generated code from managed runtime systems for heterogeneous hardware and GPUs. For now, it is important to understand how control flow divergence is handled on GPUs and why it can impact performance.

To better understand how GPUs handle control flow, let's take a look at an example. Since we haven't explained the programming models yet, we will use an example in C code. The following code snippet shows a parallel kernel that traverses the input data set (using a thread identifier) that checks whether a value is equal to one. If it is true, the output value is set to 100. Otherwise, the output is set to 50.

```
1   i = thread_id();
2   bool condition = (input[i] == 1);
3   if (condition) {
4       output[i] = 100;
5   } else {
6       output[i] = 50;
7   }
```

For this example let's assume that we are running on a GPU with a warp equal to four threads. Additionally, let's also assume that half of the input values are equal to one, and they are alternate between 0 and 1 (e.g., using an input vector with the

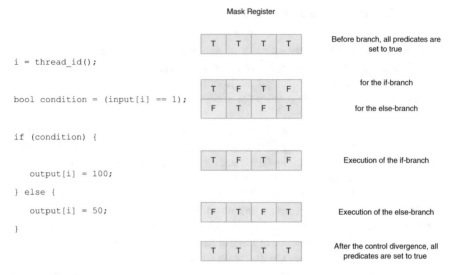

Fig. 2.13 Example of control-flow divergence on a GPU architecture

values 1, 0, 1, 0). Each GPU thread executes the code for a particular data item from the input data set.

Figure 2.13 shows a representation between the code and the register mask within the GPU. Before entering the branch and evaluating the condition, all predicates values are set to true. When the condition is evaluated, the register mask is set to true for those values that met the condition; thus, take the if-branch. The rest of the predicated values are set to false. This means that, the GPU, even though it will run the if-branch for all threads, it will not set the output values, because they are predicated. Similarly, the else-branch is executed and set for the values from the register mask that are not predicated. Finally, once the control flow converges again, the register mask is set to true for all values and the execution continues in a lock step for all the threads for the next SIMT instruction.

2.7.9   Real-World GPU Architectures

Now that we have explained how GPUs work and how execution, memory, and synchronization work, let's take a look at two real-world GPUs. The goal of this exercise is to map the concepts explained in the previous sections with the real compute microarchitectures. This will provide a full picture of the GPU architectures, and then we can start explaining, in more detail, how GPUs are programmed. Note that, as we have explained in the introduction, although we focus on the GPU compute architectures, similar principles apply for other types of accelerators, such as FPGAs, especially when programming these devices using a common parallel programming model such as OpenCL.

In this section, we will explain two GPU microarchitectures from different vendors. We will show the differences and the common parts in the hardware design, and reason about how small differences can influence performance.

NVIDIA GPUs: Ada Microarchitecture

The NVIDIA Ada microarchitecture [102] is the latest GPU architecture generation at the time of writing this book. The Ada microarchitecture implementation on the GeForce RTX 4090 GPU is considered one of the most powerful consumer GPUs in the market due to its peak performance for computing, rendering, and Deep Learning capabilities. The RTX 4090 features the AD102 GPU as shown in Fig. 2.14.

The NVIDIA RTX 4090 GPU contains 144 SMs with a total of 18432 CUDA cores for the whole GPU. Besides, it contains 144 Ray-Tracing (RT) cores, 576 Tensor Cores (TC), and 576 Texture Units (TU). The GPU is divided into 12 clusters (Graphics Processing Clusters). In turn, each cluster contains a set of 12 SMs. The RTX 4090 GPU also contains a shared L2 cache for all clusters and SMs within the GPU, with a size of 98304 KB.

Figure 2.15 shows the schematic of an SM of the AD102 microarchitecture. Each SM is divided into four partitions. Each partition contains 32 CUDA cores

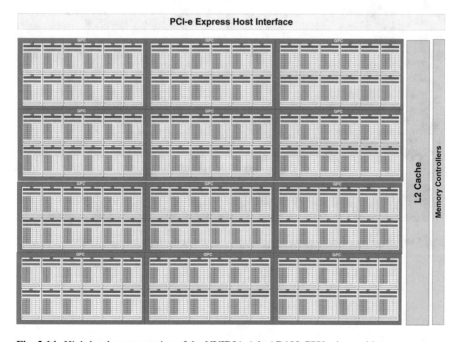

Fig. 2.14 High-level representation of the NVIDIA Ada AD102 GPU microarchitecture

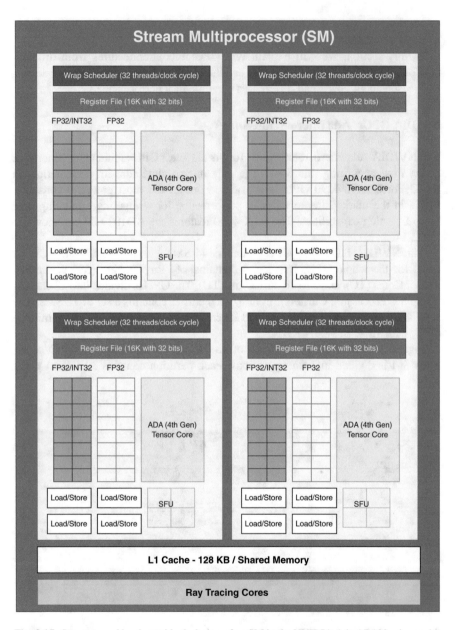

Fig. 2.15 Structure and hardware block-design of an SM in the NVIDIA Ada AD102 microarchitecture

(16 of then with the capability of performing integer arithmetic—INT32—and 32 of them with the capability of performing floating point operations in FP32). In addition, each SM contains two units to perform FP64. Thus, in this type of GPUs it is possible to operate with FP64 with a performance penalty. CPU architecture usually offers the same peak performance (FLOPS) when running FP32 and FP64. However, on GPU architectures, this is not usually the norm. In the case of the RTX 4090, the performance of FP64 is 1/64 the peak performance of FP32. Note also that, other GPUs, e.g., Apple M1/M2 Silicon, do not contain hardware to perform FP64.

Going back to the SM architecture design on the RTX 4090, each SM also contains its own register file (set of private registers) and a warp scheduler able to dispatch 32 threads per clock cycle.

Besides the general purpose FP32 and INT32 capabilities, the AD102 GPU microarchitecture also includes four tensor cores per SM (Ada 4th Generation Tensor Core from the Fig. 2.15). Each SM also contains a shared L1 cache for shared memory. Note that current GPU L1 cache is not coherent, and, as we will see in Sect. 2.7.6, programmers need to add synchronization primitives and barriers to keep memory consistency. Finally, each SM partition contains four load/store blocks and one special function unit (SFU) which is used to process graphics instructions.

As we can see, most of the chip is, in fact, dedicated to compute, rather than control (e.g, no branch predictor, speculation, and cache coherence). From this type of compute architecture, we can see the potential of running many concurrent threads on the GPU, with the intention of maximizing throughput.

Intel Xe-HPG Alchemist (ARC) Discrete GPU

The Alchemist GPU is the latest discrete GPU microarchitecture from Intel, at the time of writing this book. The Alchemist features the Xe-HPG (High Performance Gaming) core, and it is an evolution of the Execution Unit (EU) from the Intel Integrated graphics (iGPUs).

Similarly to the NVIDIA AD102 microarchitecture, the Intel Xe-HPG features specialized hardware, not just for compute and rendering graphics, but also for specialized fixed functions for ray tracing, super sampling, and deep learning. For the purpose of this book, we will focus on the computing components. However, for curious readers, we recommend taking a deep look into other hardware components such as the Super Sampling and Deep Learning inference cores [11].

Intel released the first ARC discrete GPUs in October 2022 [10] with the introduction of the Xe-HPG (High Performance Gaming) GPU organization. The microarchitecture released for these graphics cards is the ARC GPU model. The Xe-HPG contains two important hardware components: the render slice, and the Xe-Core (the heart of this GPU microarchitecture).

Figure 2.16 shows an overview of the Arc GPU microarchitecture found in the Arc 770 GPU (a high-performance gaming GPU). This GPU contains eight rendering slices and each slice contains four Xe-Cores. The Arc 770 GPU contains

Fig. 2.16 Overview of the Alchemist Xe-HPG microarchitecture of Intel discrete GPUs

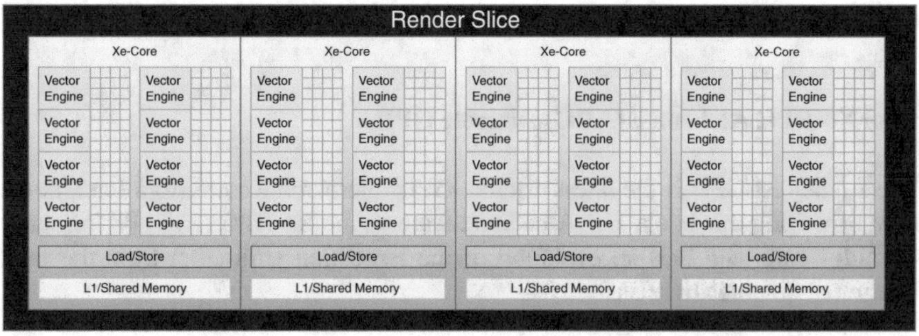

Fig. 2.17 GPU microarchitecture of the Xe-Core from the Intel Arc microarchitecture shipped with the Arc 770 GPU

up to 16GB of GDDR6 memory offering up to 560 GB/s [71]. In addition, it contains an L2 cache shared across all rendering slides of up to 16384 KBs. Each rendering slice contains a set of fixed functions to perform real-time ray tracing (similar to the NVIDIA AD102 GPU that we saw previously).

Figure 2.17 shows the render slice in more detail. A render slice is similar to a raster engine from the NVIDIA GPU microarchitecture that we saw in the previous section. The render slice in the Intel ARC contains four Xe-Cores. Each Xe-Core on the top-of-the-line gaming GPU (Arc 770) contains 16 vector units (XVE) and 16 matrix units (XMX) per XVE unit. In addition, each Xe-Core contains a load/store unit and an L1 cache for accessing shared data within the Xe-Core. The Arc 770 GPU contains, in total, 32 Xe-Cores for rendering and parallel processing.

In terms of performance, the Arc 770 GPU features a peak performance of up to 19.66 TFLOPS in floating point single precision (FP32). Note that this GPU does not support FP64. This is something to keep in mind from the programming perspective, because if we need to compute with FP64 (e.g., using the double data type in programming languages such as Java), there is no hardware support, and most likely, we will get a runtime exception (from the GPU driver) indicating that this type of operations is not available for the GPU being used. We will discuss this in more detail in Chap. 3 when we discuss programming models for GPUs.

Interestingly, the Arc 770 GPU offers up to 137.6 TOP of peak performance using FP16 and XMX (matrix) operations, and up to 276.2 TOPs of peak performance using integer arithmetic of eight bits (INT8) with matrix operations (XMX) [11].

Similarly to the NVIDIA GPUs, the Intel Arc 770 dedicates most of the chip area to compute, rather than cache and control. This design helps to achieve high throughput of applications, if the input applications follow particular patterns. In the next section, we will discuss, based on the hardware design that we have presented, what GPUs are good for, and what types of applications should be avoided when running on this type of accelerator.

2.8   What Are GPUs Suitable for?

We will briefly introduce what types of applications are beneficial, in terms of performance, to run on GPUs. We will elaborate further on this topic in Chap. 3 when we will explain how the GPU programming models work. Nevertheless, based on what we have seen regarding the compute architecture of the GPUs, we can start drawing some first insights.

GPU hardware is optimized for high throughput. In order to hide latencies, GPUs provide hardware mechanisms to run hundreds, or even thousands of threads in parallel with specialized functions for ray tracing and AI workloads. Due to this design, GPUs are generally ideal at exploiting high level of parallelism, especially when each thread is able to perform the computation without any communication or interaction with any other thread.

These types of applications are classified as embarrassingly parallel and have no data dependencies between different threads. This type of applications might seem a bit restrictive; however, many application domains contain such application patterns. Examples of such domains are: Deep Learning and AI, which use matrix multiplications and matrix operations (usually independent per thread), Physics simulations, such as NBody, math simulation and Fintech, such as Montecarlo-based applications, etc.

Furthermore, GPUs can execute other types of applications or software patterns very efficiently. For example, they can perform really fast reductions, stencils, scans, etc. Usually, GPU programming models offer intrinsics and low-level fast libraries to perform this type of operations efficiently. This helps developers to cover a wider spectrum of applications that can be parallelized and executed efficiently on these accelerators. One important thing to keep in mind is that, although GPUs can not be used to program everything (at least efficiently), GPUs can be used for a wide spectrum of applications.

Although it is not advised, developers can also run single-thread applications on GPUs. However, due to the lack of hardware control for fast single-threaded execution, such as speculation, branch predictor, etc., single-threaded GPU computation generally runs slower than on a CPU. Additionally, GPUs do not run a single thread in isolation, but rather in a block of usually 32 or 64 threads in parallel (e.g., a warp). As a general rule of thumb, GPUs need many threads to run efficiently (usually more than 1000 threads). This might not be always the case, but, in general, developers map a function to be computed over a data item with a GPU thread.

In addition, developers must pay special attention to the cost of offloading. This is the time that takes for an application to start and move data from the host (a CPU) to the device (a GPU). Computation is not initiated instantly, and data transfers as well as kernel compilation take time. Thus, developers must factor in the time to do all these operations in order to initiate the computation and obtain the desired results. What this means is that, even though some applications might be suitable for acceleration, if the data transfer takes more time than the actual computation, developers might not obtain the desired performance.

One way to approach GPU computation and obtain parallel code in an easier way is through the identification of parallel patterns (or skeletons) [70] in the code. In a nutshell, what we usually try to do is to look for patterns in the code. Patterns help us organize the code, understand its behavior, and, in many cases, decouple implementation details from the behavior and the semantics of the application. As such, there is also a list of parallel patterns, such as map, reduce and stencil. GPUs can be used to exploit all these parallel patterns to various degrees.

2.9 Summary

This chapter gave the necessary background on computer architecture in order to understand how hardware accelerators are programmed and execute code. While this book focuses on high-level programming languages and managed runtime systems, programming accelerators usually requires deep understanding of the architecture underneath. This chapter focused on GPU architectures as a representative accelerator type. Besides, it highlighted the main differences between CPU architectures and GPUs, and explained the GPU execution model. Since, this chapter is geared towards readers that are new to GPU architecture and GPU programming, it introduced the terms related to the GPU architecture and explained the similarities and differences between different GPU vendors. Readers will find supplementary exercises to reflect on the material discussed in this chapter [14].

The next chapter will introduce and expand on how GPUs can be programmed via mainstream parallel programming models, such as OpenCL and CUDA.

Chapter 3
Heterogeneous Programming Models

3.1 Introduction to Heterogeneous Programming Models

A programming model is a set of defined guidelines that must be followed by programmers to achieve the required functionality. That functionality can be expressed by questions, such as *"how to communicate with a hardware device?"*, *"how to transfer data between a hardware device and the main CPU?"*, or *"how to express parallelism in my application code?"*. To address those questions, the programming models are designed as an abstraction layer over hardware details (i.e., interconnects, registers, etc.), and therefore, they can increase the productivity of programmers who do not need to consider the hardware complexity when building their programs. Without the existence of the heterogeneous programming models, programmers would be forced to assimilate knowledge spanning from computer micro-architecture and hardware interconnects to operating systems and memory management.

Therefore, all programming models for heterogeneous architectures have as a common objective to offer **a unified set of rules (i.e., the specification)** that must be followed by programmers, along with **an API** to access heterogeneous hardware from their software codebase. The specifications are being defined and maintained either by a single vendor or a group of vendors in a standardized manner. For instance, NVIDIA is the creator of the CUDA programming model which includes an API and a system platform that together define a programming path for accessing NVIDIA GPUs. Similarly, AMD and Intel offer their own programming platforms, namely AMD ROCm and Intel oneAPI, respectively. On the other hand, OpenCL, Vulkan, and SYCL are standards that are being maintained by the Khronos Group [86]; a consortium of organizations working together to maintain and advance those standards. The specifications of those standards are used as drivers for the implementation of the vendor-specific software platforms. For example, the Intel oneAPI DPC++ is an open-source LLVM-based technology

© The Author(s), under exclusive license to Springer Nature Switzerland AG 2024
J. Fumero et al., *Programming Heterogeneous Hardware via Managed Runtime Systems*, SpringerBriefs in Computer Science,
https://doi.org/10.1007/978-3-031-49559-5_3

implementation of SYCL. The next section will describe the landscape of the state-of-the-art programming models for heterogeneous hardware accelerators.

3.2 Landscape of Programming Models

In the realm of heterogeneous programming models, there have been numerous platforms implemented to offer the abstraction that programmers seek to increase the productivity of the development of parallel software implementations. Therefore, all hardware vendors are providing software platforms that comprise various software technologies, such as compilers, and auxiliary software toolkits (e.g., profilers, debuggers, converters). Figure 3.1 illustrates the programming language, compiler infrastructure, and the code format of the generated code for the state-of-the art heterogeneous computing platforms. NVIDIA CUDA, Intel oneAPI, AMD ROCm, and Apple Metal are prime examples of such software platforms. The supported programming languages of those platforms are extensions to C and C++. To this extent, they all provide a compiler implementation that is based on Clang/LLVM compiler infrastructure. Thus, Clang is used as a compiler front-end for the supported programming languages, and subsequently the LLVM Intermediate Representation is employed to lower the user programs from a high level form into a low-level one; that is architecture dependent. Subsequently, the lowered representation of the user programs is used for the emission of the machine code, that corresponds to the compiler backend that is supported by each compiler. For instance, the Intel oneAPI platform can generate OpenCL C, SPIR-V binary, or even CUDA PTX. The AMD ROCm platform generates HIP, OpenCL C, and OpenMP. NVIDIA CUDA and Apple Metal comprise proprietary compiler implementations (i.e., nvcc and metal) that emit vendor-specific GPU binary code (i.e., CUDA PTX and Metal GPU machine code).

The large number of software platforms has been the springboard of a competition that started at the beginning of 2010 between the hardware vendors.

	DPC++	C/C++	CUDA C, C++, FORTRAN	HIP C++	Metal Shading Language (MSL)
SDK	Intel oneAPI	OpenCL SDK	NVIDIA CUDA	AMD ROCm	macOSx SDK
Compiler	LLVM (dpc++)	LLVM	LLVM (nvcc)	LLVM (hipcc)	Metal Compiler
Generated Code	SPIR-V/ VULKAN	OpenCL C/ SPIR-V	CUDA PTX / OpenCL C	HIP	Metal GPU Code

Fig. 3.1 Classification of heterogeneous programming models based on the hardware vendors

All hardware vendors have been focusing on enhancing their provided software infrastructure to attract more developers, thereby forcing some software ecosystems (e.g., Deep Learning and Artificial Intelligence (AI) frameworks) to lock into their solutions. Vendor lock-in posed constraints into software programmers and hindered them from migrating their software to different software platforms; something that could offer portability to hardware offered by various vendors.

In recent years, undeniably NVIDIA has been the most dominant hardware vendor in the AI application domain, followed by AMD and Intel. Lately, both AMD and Intel have intensified their efforts to bridge this gap. Hence, they have enhanced their software platforms with programmer friendly tools, such as the AMD HIPify (https://rocm.docs.amd.com/projects/HIPIFY/en/latest/index.html) and the Intel oneAPI SYCLomatic [103], that facilitate the migration of existing software applications implemented with NVIDIA CUDA to their hardware.

3.3 Mapping of Programming Models and Hardware Devices

Every programming model shown in Fig. 3.1 targets a particular set of hardware devices and architectures. Table 3.1 presents all supported hardware types per programming model. For instance, OpenCL is a specification supported by different hardware vendors, including enterprises shipping multi-core CPUs, GPUs, FPGAs, and other types of accelerators, such as Digital Signal Processors (DSPs). Vulkan is an open standard for three-dimensional graphics and computing, and it is supported by numerous GPU vendors, including NVIDIA, AMD, and Apple. The oneAPI specification is an open, cross-industry multi-vendor programming model that aims to unify and provide a common way to program multiple hardware architectures. Recently, the oneAPI specification joined the Unified Acceleration Foundation [87]. Unlike OpenCL and Vulkan which are open standards, hardware vendors also offer their proprietary programming models which are tailored to their hardware offerings. NVIDIA CUDA is the most dominant programming models for programming NVIDIA GPUs. AMD HIP and Apple Metal are also prime examples of proprietary heterogeneous programming models.

Table 3.1 Support of hardware devices per heterogeneous programming model

	Multi-core CPUs	GPUs	FPGAs	Other
OpenCL	Yes	Yes	Yes	Yes
Vulkan	No	Yes	No	No
CUDA	No	Yes (NVIDIA)	No	No
oneAPI	Yes (Intel)	Yes (Intel)	Yes (Intel)	No
AMD HIP	No	Yes (AMD)	No	No
Apple meta GPU machine code	Yes (Apple)	Yes (Apple)	No	No

3.4   Fundamental Building Blocks of a Programming Model

At this point, you may wonder *"what is the difference between a programming model and a standardized specification?"* and *"why the same name is used sometimes for both the model and the format file of the parallel code?"*. To clarify those questions, we must distinguish that a programming model is not only the parallel implementation of the user code. In some cases, the name given to a programming model, has been also given to the code format that is supported, thereby creating confusion. For example, the OpenCL programming model is not the same as the OpenCL C code that is generated by a compiler or is written by a programmer.

A programming model is more than just the generated code as it also contains a runtime system that is accessed by programmers via a Software Development Kit (SDK). The runtime system implements the specification of the execution and memory models. Besides the runtime system, a vendor implementation might include a driver to handle the compilation and execution of the target functions (kernels) on the device. Figure 3.2 presents a simplified overview of the structure within a heterogeneous computing platform.

In this section, we will dive into the runtime system of a programming model, and we will explain the fundamental blocks that enable a programmer to access and execute on a heterogeneous hardware accelerator at runtime. To narrow down the scope and facilitate readers to comprehend how programming models operate, we will focus on the OpenCL and CUDA programming models for the remainder of this chapter.

The OpenCL runtime system that is packaged within a heterogeneous computing platform (e.g., Intel oneAPI, NVIDIA CUDA) is often provided by vendors as a library (libOpenCL.so). That library is linked by OpenCL user programs. That library is not an OpenCL implementation itself, but it maps to the actual implementation that is being implemented by vendors via the OpenCL Installable Client Driver (ICD). An ICD loader can be provided by an Operating System distribution (e.g., the Ubuntu opencl-icd package) or it can be built using OS-compliant building

Fig. 3.2 An overview of the inner blocks of a heterogeneous computing platform

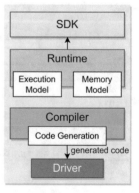

tools. The loader is responsible for loading all OpenCL implementations that are available on the system and exporting the implemented OpenCL API entry points to the programmers. For example, programmers who want to write an OpenCL program that offloads the execution of a compute function on an accelerator, must include the OpenCL header files in their program. The header files will enable them to see the OpenCL API points in their program. When the program will be compiled and linked, the OpenCL library that is being provided by the vendors will be used to link with the vendor-specific implementation of the OpenCL specification. To write a program that adheres to the OpenCL programming model (and any other programming model), someone needs to understand first the execution model that must be followed. For instance, a program cannot directly offload a compute function on a GPU device, if the target device has not been identified by the program and several internal data structures have not been initialized to operate for the target device. Thus, the OpenCL execution model comprises four main stages. The first stage employs API calls for the initialization of the internal data structures of the programming models (e.g., command queue, context, data buffers, kernel, etc.—see Sect. 3.4.1). The second stage employs a series of API functions that are responsible for transferring the input data of the compute function to the suitable memory segment of the target accelerator (Sect. 3.4.2). The third stage launches the execution of a compute function on the accelerator (Sect. 3.4.3), while also configuring the grid of threads to be launched. Finally, the fourth stage returns the result of the computed data back to the user program (Sect. 3.4.4). Each stage will be discussed in the following paragraphs.

3.4.1   Initialization of Data Structures

Context and Command Queues

The primary data structures that are created first are the ***context*** and the ***command queues***. The former is used to access a device driver for each device that is bound on a *context*, while the latter serves as a direct channel between the programmer and the driver. Thus, on the one side the programmer feeds commands into a *command queue*, and on the other side the driver fetches the commands and executes them one by one. In some cases, the *command queues* can be configured to be utilized out-of-order and can be used to create dependencies between different commands. However, this might not be the default case.

The terminology of the *context* and the *command queue* is used in several specifications, such as the OpenCL API, the Intel oneAPI, and Intel Level Zero API. The CUDA Driver API employs also the term of the *context*, but it uses the term of the CUDA stream for the data structure that is semantically equivalent to the *command queue*. Similarly, the CUDA Runtime API, which is placed one level higher than the corresponding Driver API, removes the explicit usage of both data structures as a means to increase the abstraction to programmers. Thus, a default CUDA *context* and CUDA stream are created during the first API call in the CUDA runtime library. Similarly, the AMD HIP Runtime API (part of the AMD ROCm platform) exposes a macro, namely *hipStreamDefault*, to perform the same functionality. The Apple Metal API exposes a data structure, namely *MTLDevice*, which encloses the ability to create and assign a *command queue* to a program as well as other operations related to transferring data and data synchronization.

Kernels

From the programmers' perspective, the most important term in heterogeneous programming is the kernel. A kernel is defined as a piece of code, that corresponds to a function/procedure that is to be offloaded for execution on a heterogeneous device. The term kernel has been adopted by OpenCL, CUDA, and other programming models. A kernel is composed of two parts: (i) the declaration of the kernel along with the input and output arguments of the kernel, and (ii) the body of the kernel that contains the statements that specify what the kernel does.

Declaration of a Kernel

In OpenCL, programmers can declare the functions that belong to their applications and are going to be executed on OpenCL-compatible devices by using the `__kernel` (or `kernel`) qualifier. Occasionally, a programmer may employ some specific attributes that should follow the kernel qualifier in the declaration of a kernel function.

The attributes can be used as a hint to the compiler to optimize the generated code. Table 3.2 presents the supported attributes in OpenCL. The first attribute is a signal to the compiler that the most operations in the `__kernel` function are explicitly vectorized using a particular vector type of the supported types. In the `__attribute__((vec_type_hint(<type>)))` qualifier, the argument `<type>` can be any built-in vector data type [61]. The last two attributes are used to declare the size of a work group that is intended to be used for execution.

The remaining part that completes the declaration of a kernel is similar to the declaration of a regular C/C++ function. Hence, the programmer must specify a return type that corresponds to the output of the kernel. The return type of an OpenCL or CUDA kernel is `void`, since both programming models force

Table 3.2 OpenCL attributes used as compiler hints

`__attribute__((vec_type_hint(<type>)))`	Declaration that the kernel contains operations that use the OpenCL vector types.
`__attribute__((work_group_size_hint(X, Y, Z)))`	Declaration of the work group size that can be used for the kernel.
`__attribute__((reqd_work_group_size(X, Y, Z)))`	Declaration of the local work group size that must be used for the kernel. The size must be the same as the local_work_size argument to clEnqueueNDRangeKernel.

Table 3.3 Qualifiers in OpenCL and CUDA

	OpenCL	CUDA
Kernel	__kernel/kernel	__global__
Constant memory	__constant/constant	__constant__
Global memory	__global/global	None
Global variable	__global/global	__device__
Shared memory	__local/local	__shared__
Private memory	__private/private	None

programmers to obtain results via data transfers. The result of a kernel must be transferred from the accelerator back to the host side, and therefore it must be written in a memory object. More information regarding the transferring of data will be provided in "pages 44 and 47 in this chapter". The declaration of the return type is followed by the declaration of the name of the kernel and the list of arguments that are specified within parentheses.

An argument can be a pointer to an address space of the device memory, or a variable of a primitive type that is stored in an address space. An address space corresponds to a memory region (i.e., global, local, private) as discussed in Sect. 2.7.6. Table 3.3 presents the qualifiers of OpenCL and CUDA that must be used to declare the address space that is pointed by an argument pointer. Data residing in global memory are visible to all threads within a kernel. For example, if an argument of an OpenCL kernel points to the address space in the global memory, it is defined with the __global qualifier.

> Note that the list of arguments must be aligned with the actual arguments that are explicitly passed by a programmer to a kernel at runtime.

Body of the Kernel

The body of a kernel is the code segment that is executed by each thread; or work-item, as referred in the OpenCL terminology. That code segment contains the declaration of variables which reside in the private memory, and therefore they are in the scope of the actual thread. Furthermore, a kernel may access data stored in the global memory or allocate a memory region in the shared memory (also known as local memory) to be shared across different threads. The shared memory is used to offer faster memory accesses than global memory, similar to the cache memory of the CPU. However, the simultaneous access of data by different threads can result in race conditions and incorrect results due to the absence of memory coherence (see Sect. 2.7.7). To prevent the synchronization issue, a barrier mechanism is provided by OpenCL and other heterogeneous programming models. In OpenCL, programmers must explicitly use a barrier function in their programs to ensure that all work-items that belong to the same work group will await [66]. The function can be used with a configuration flag (i.e., CLK_GLOBAL_MEM_FENCE or

CLK_LOCAL_MEM_FENCE) to apply a memory fence over the global or shared memory, respectively. Besides the declaration of data stored in the private and shared memory, a kernel may contain various operations over the input data.

One group of operations regards arithmetic or logical calculations, and they can be also expressed explicitly by typing an operator [63] or implicitly by invoking a built-in function [64]. The former statement is common for standard operations such as addition, subtraction, division, multiplication, etc., while the latter is employed to perform more complex operations such as mathematical functions (e.g., cos, sin, log, pow, etc.).

A second group of operations regards the loading and storing of data from various address spaces as per the specified argument declaration. Those operations can be handled by pointers or by dedicated built-in functions that facilitate the operation over vector types. OpenCL offers several load and store functions (e.g., vloadn and vstoren) for data of various vector types. The functions provide support for the basic primitive data types, and n corresponds to the actual element size of the vectors and it can be 2, 3, 4, 8, or 16.

Data Buffers
Typically, to transfer data from the host (i.e., the CPU) to an accelerator, dedicated data structures are used known as **buffers**. Both OpenCL and CUDA employ buffers, as allocated memory regions, that can be accessed by the host and the accelerator devices in order to transfer data. For example, in OpenCL an OpenCL buffer is created via the clCreateBuffer call [65]. In CUDA, cudaMalloc is used to allocate a memory space on the device memory [67]. Thus, the host writes input data to the buffers. Once the data is written in the device memory, the kernel is ready to consume it and produce the result data. The result data is written by the kernel in an allocated memory space on the device memory, which can be associated with the same buffer or a separate buffer allocated only for the result. In turn, the host reads the result data via the corresponding data buffer.

Please note that OpenCL and CUDA programmers are responsible for allocating/deallocating those memory regions, as well as for keeping consistency between the host memory (i.e., the main memory) and the device memory (i.e., global memory on the device—DRAM).

3.4.2 Transferring of Input Data

Following the previous paragraphs that described the basic internal blocks of heterogeneous programming models, we can now elaborate on the remaining stages of the OpenCL execution model. The next stage concerns the operation of transferring input data from the main memory of the CPU to the DRAM memory on the accelerator device (e.g., GPU). That operation is expressed as a command that copies the data to an allocated data buffer (e.g., an OpenCL buffer created via clCreateBuffer). Then the command is enqueued in a command queue via a specific API function call, such as clEnqueueWriteBuffer. That function call exposes numerous configuration parameters to programmers, including the declaration of whether the operation is blocking or non-blocking, the size of data being written in bytes, the offset in bytes in the buffer object to write the data to, and finally the declaration of any events that have to be completed before the execution of that command. Finally, the function call returns a specific event object that identifies that specific command, and a status that characterizes the successful or erroneous execution of the function call. The events are used to query the status of any command issued in the command queue.

The operation of writing data to the memory of the accelerator device is necessary for devices that do not support the sharing of the virtual address space between the CPU and the accelerator. This feature has been implemented by NVIDIA and Intel as the Unified Memory [52] or Unified Shared Memory [53, 54], respectively, and enables the CPU and the accelerator devices to share an address space. Thus, data can be accessed without requiring an explicit copy from the programmer, as described in the previous paragraph with the clEnqueueWriteBuffer function call. Instead, the migration of data from the CPU to the accelerator is automatically handled by the device driver. At this point, we will not dive into that feature as it is a vendor-specific functionality. Hence, we point readers to the relevant sources [52, 54–57].

3.4.3   Execution of a Compute Function (Kernel)

Launching a kernel for execution on an accelerator device is a process performed by the actual program. A kernel can be compiled ahead of time or just in time, based on the characteristics of the applications or the targeted hardware platform. For example, launching a kernel on an FPGA can take few hours due to the compilation time in the High-Level Synthesis (HLS) tools that transform the OpenCL C code to binary machine code. Thus, it is common to launch kernels that have been compiled ahead of time on FPGAs. For GPUs, the driver is invoked at runtime to compile and link an executable of a kernel at runtime.

Figure 3.3 presents the four steps that are defined in OpenCL prior to launching a kernel on an accelerator. The first step (Step 1) concerns the creation of a *cl_program* which is an object that has been designed to represent one or multiple kernels to be launched. OpenCL 3.0 supports the creation of a program from three different types of inputs, and it exposes a dedicated function call accordingly:

- The creation of a program from source code via clCreateProgramWithSource function.

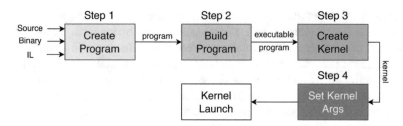

Fig. 3.3 The workflow of the four steps that programmers must carry out before launching a kernel

- The creation of a program from binary code via the `clCreateProgramWithBinary` function.
- The creation of a program from an implementation-defined intermediate language or a block of memory that contains SPIR-V binary code via the `clCreateProgram- WithIL` function.

Once a program has been created the `clBuildProgram` function is invoked to build the program (Step 2). That function is responsible for compiling and linking the executable of a program that may contain one or multiple kernels.

The third step (Step 3) creates a kernel object to launch a specific kernel from an executable. A kernel object is obtained from the executable of a *cl_program* and is tied to a specific function name that has been previously declared by using the `__kernel` qualifier in the kernel body (see Sect. 3.4.1). The function call that is employed by programmers to create a kernel for launching is `clCreateKernel`, and it returns a valid non-zero kernel object. Furthermore, a set of possible erroneous codes may be returned to indicate whether a kernel name or a program executable has been invalid, or there has been a failure to allocate resources on the device, etc.

Once the three steps are executed with no resulting failures, programmers are ready to pass the arguments of the kernel to be launched (Step 4). The `clSetKernelArg` function is invoked to set the value for each argument of a kernel. That function call uses the created kernel object and the index of the argument. Additionally, in case that an argument refers to an allocated data space, the argument size is passed along with a pointer to the OpenCL data buffers (i.e., type is `cl_mem` as defined in OpenCL). Alternatively, if an argument corresponds to a primitive variable of a scalar data type, the address of the variable is passed along with the respective size in bytes. A list of the supported OpenCL scalar data types is available here [62].

Once the kernel object has been created and every kernel argument has been set, the command for launching is ready to be enqueued in the command queue. The OpenCL command used for launching kernels is `clEnqueueNDRangeKernel`, and accepts as inputs the command queue, the kernel object, as well as the number of events and the list of events that must be completed before the execution of the command. Additionally, programmers must configure as inputs the global and local work group sizes as well as the number of dimensions that will be used. The sizes of the global and local work groups correspond to the size of the blocks of threads that compose the overall grid that the kernel instance is executed. In addition, the number of dimensions depends on the range of the deployed work groups and must be greater than zero and less than or equal to three. More information about the grid, the block and the dimensions is already provided in Sect. 2.7.5. Finally, the command returns a status that indicates the success or failure of the command.

In the scenario that a kernel is configured to be launched in a grid of one dimension with the size of the global and local work groups being one, the clEnqueueNDRangeKernel is equivalent to calling clEnqueueTask. That command is a simplified version that accepts as inputs only the command queue, the kernel object, and the list of events on which it is dependent.

> The size of work groups must be the same with the configuration of the attributes used in the declaration of the kernel (see the relevant paragraph in Sect. 3.4.1). Additionally, the launching and the actual execution of a kernel may not happen instantly. The reason is that the clEnqueueNDRangeKernel command enqueues the kernel to be executed in a command queue, and subsequently the driver dispatches the command from the command queue.

3.4.4   Transferring of Result Data

The step that follows the execution of a kernel on an accelerator is transferring the data that have been created as a result of the computation performed within the kernel. That step can be considered as the reverse operation of the data movement described in Sect. 3.4.2. Thus, we will assume that the memory address space between the CPU and the targeted accelerator device is not shared.

The operation of transferring result data from the DRAM memory on the accelerator device to the main memory of the CPU is expressed as a command enqueued in a command queue via a specific API function call, such as clEnqueueReadBuffer. The arguments of that function call are the same with the corresponding arguments of the clEnqueueWriteBuffer function. In particular, the declaration whether the operation is blocking or non-blocking, the size of data being read in bytes, along with the offset in bytes to read the data from, and the declaration of any events on which this operation has a dependency. For instance, the transferring of the result data is dependent on the event that is tied to the execution of the kernel, as the computation performed by the kernel must be completed before transferring the data. Otherwise, the result transferred to the CPU will be incorrect. Additionally, the read function call contains an argument of the event object that is returned, and returns a status that indicates the successful or erroneous execution of the function call. The only difference between the two function calls is that the pointer specified by the programmer should point to the address space that has been allocated in the CPU main memory to store the outcome of the accelerator device.

3.5   Example of Using Heterogeneous Programming Models

Now that the fundamental blocks of the programming models have been described, it is time to present how to apply them in practice. In this section, we assume that the Software Development Kits (SDKs) of OpenCL and CUDA are already installed in the system, and our goal is to showcase how to write a program in C++ and employ a heterogeneous programming model to offload a computation on a hardware accelerator, such as a GPU. In particular, Sect. 3.5.1 presents an example that applies the OpenCL model, whereas Sect. 3.5.2 presents a program that follows the CUDA model. For simplification, both programs perform the same computation (i.e., matrix multiplication) which is a fundamental operation found at the heart of image recognition, speech recognition, compression and use cases in the AI domain. The source code of both programs is available in GitHub as open-source software [59].

3.5.1   An Example of an OpenCL Program

To facilitate readers to comprehend the transformation steps of an ordinary compute function to a parallel implementation in OpenCL, we present the nominal C implementation of matrix multiplication in Listing 3.1. The code snippet in Listing 3.1 is written in C and will be considered hereafter as the baseline sequential implementation of our example.

Listing 3.1 Sequential implementation of matrix multiplication in C

```
1   void matrixMultiplication(float* A, float* B, float* C,
2       int sizeX, int sizeY, int width) {
3       for (int i = 0; i < sizeX; i++) {
4           for (int j = 0; j < sizeY; j++) {
5               float sum = 0.0f;
6               for (int k = 0; k < width; k++) {
7                   sum += A[k * sizeX + i] * B[j*width + k];
8               }
9               C[j * sizeX + i] = sum;
10          }
11      }
12  }
```

The OpenCL program of the matrix multiplication example comprises two source files. The first file (i.e., namely host.cpp) is the part of the program executed on the CPU and it is written in C++, whereas the second file (i.e., namely kernel.cl)

contains the OpenCL C function that is the parallel implementation of matrix multiplication (Listing 3.2). Lines 1-2 show the declaration of the kernel, while the rest of the lines represent the kernel body. The kernel body replaces the indices of the two outermost loops (lines 3-4 in Listing 3.1) with the thread identifiers that correspond to the two grid dimensions, as shown in lines 3-4 in Listing 3.2.

Listing 3.2 OpenCL C kernel for matrix multiplication

```
1   __kernel void matrixMultiplication(__global float* A, __global float* B,
2       __global float* C, int sizeX, int sizeY, int width) {
3       int i = get_global_id(0);
4       int j = get_global_id(1);
5
6       float sum = 0.0f;
7       for (int k = 0; k < width; k++) {
8           sum += A[k * sizeX + i] * B[j * width + k];
9       }
10      C[j * sizeX + i] = sum;
11  }
```

The host code of the program contains some auxiliary tasks and some primary tasks. The auxiliary tasks contain the discovery of the available platforms, the initialization of the input data as well as the validation of the result data from the GPU. The primary tasks correspond to the material discussed in this chapter and they are executed in five steps, as follows:

1. Initialize the OpenCL data structures (i.e., context, command queue) along with the necessary data buffers, as discussed in Sect. 3.4.1.
2. Transfer input data from host to device, as explained in Sect. 3.4.2.
3. Create a kernel object from the OpenCL C source that is included in the kernel file. To create the kernel object, we followed the workflow prior to launching a kernel as described in Sect. 3.4.3.
4. Launch the execution of the created kernel object.
5. Transfer result data from device to host, as explained in Sect. 3.4.4.

Step 1. Initialize the OpenCL Data Structures and Data Buffers

The first step is to create and define the OpenCL data structures (i.e., context, command queue) and the necessary data buffers. Listing 3.3 presents the creation of the OpenCL context and command queue that will be used by our program to enqueue various OpenCL commands. Listing 3.4 shows the creation of three OpenCL data buffers in lines 2-10 which are also mapped to the CPU address space (lines 16-21).

Listing 3.3 Initialization of OpenCL data structures

```
1   int initializeDataStructures() {
2       cl_int status;
3       context = clCreateContext(NULL, numDevices, devices, NULL, NULL, &status);
4       if (status != CL_SUCCESS) {
5           cout << "Error in clCreateContext" << endl;
6           return status;
7       }
8
9       commandQueue = clCreateCommandQueue(context, devices[0],
10          CL_QUEUE_PROFILING_ENABLE, &status);
11
12      if (status != CL_SUCCESS || commandQueue == NULL) {
13          cout << "Error in clCreateCommandQueue" << endl;
14          return status;
15      }
16      return status;
17  }
```

Listing 3.4 Creation of OpenCL data buffers

```
1   int createDataBuffers() {
2       cl_int status;
3       d_A = clCreateBuffer(context, CL_MEM_READ_WRITE, datasize, NULL, &status);
4       if (CL_SUCCESS != status) {
5           cout << "Error in clCreateBuffer for array d_A" << endl;
6       }
7       d_B = clCreateBuffer(context, CL_MEM_READ_WRITE, datasize, NULL, &status);
8       if (CL_SUCCESS != status) {
9           cout << "Error in clCreateBuffer for array d_B" << endl;
10      }
11      d_C = clCreateBuffer(context, CL_MEM_READ_WRITE, datasize, NULL, &status);
12      if (CL_SUCCESS != status) {
13          cout << "Error in clCreateBuffer for array d_C" << endl;
14      }
15
16      A = (float *) clEnqueueMapBuffer(commandQueue, d_A, CL_TRUE, CL_MAP_WRITE,
17                  0, datasize, 0, NULL, NULL, NULL);
18      B = (float *) clEnqueueMapBuffer(commandQueue, d_B, CL_TRUE, CL_MAP_WRITE,
19                  0, datasize, 0, NULL, NULL, NULL);
20      C = (float *) clEnqueueMapBuffer(commandQueue, d_C, CL_TRUE, CL_MAP_READ,
21                  0, datasize, 0, NULL, NULL, NULL);
22
23      return status;
24  }
```

Step 2. Transfer Input Data from Host to Device

The second step concerns the transferring of input data from host to device. Listing 3.5 shows in lines 2–5 the OpenCL commands that write the input data of matrices A and B to the global memory of the GPU device. Line 6 ensures that all commands that have been added in the command queue are issued to the device.

Listing 3.5 OpenCL commands for transferring input data from host to device

```
1  void transferInputDataToPlatform() {
2      clEnqueueWriteBuffer(commandQueue, d_A, CL_TRUE, 0, datasize, A,
3                  0, NULL, &writeEvent1);
4      clEnqueueWriteBuffer(commandQueue, d_B, CL_TRUE, 0, datasize, B,
5                  0, NULL, &writeEvent2);
6      clFlush(commandQueue);
7  }
```

Step 3. Create a Kernel Object and Set the Arguments

This step contains the steps to create a kernel object from the OpenCL C source code that is included in the kernel file. To create the kernel object, we followed the workflow that is executed prior to launching a kernel, as described in Sect. 3.4.3. We recall that the workflow comprises four steps that have been illustrated in Fig. 3.3. Listing 3.6 presents the creation of a program from source in lines 5–10 (Step 1), the building of a program in lines 11–15 (Step 2), and the creation of a kernel with name "matrixMultiplication" in lines 16–20 (Step 3). The final step that corresponds to the assignment of the arguments of the kernel is shown in Listing 3.7. The kernel has six arguments, including three pointers to data that resides in global memory and three integer values that correspond to the size of the matrices. In our example, the kernel multiplies two two-dimensional square matrices A and B, in which each dimension has the size of elements1D elements.

Listing 3.6 Creation of kernel object from source program. The code snippet implements the workflow shown in Fig. 3.3

```
1  int createKernelFromProgramSource(char* sourceFile) {
2      cl_int status;
3      // Build from source
4      source = readsource(sourceFile);
5      program = clCreateProgramWithSource(context, 1,
6                  (const char **) &source, NULL, &status);
7      if (CL_SUCCESS != status) {
8          cout << "Error in clCreateProgramWithSource" << endl;
9          return status;
10     }
11     status = clBuildProgram(program, numDevices, devices, NULL, NULL, NULL);
12     if (CL_SUCCESS != status) {
13         cout << "Error in clBuildProgram" << endl;
14         return status;
```

```
15      }
16      kernel = clCreateKernel(program, "matrixMultiplication", &status);
17      if (CL_SUCCESS != status) {
18          cout << "Error in clCreateKernel, matrixMultiplication kernel" << endl;
19          return status;
20      }
21      return status;
22  }
```

Listing 3.7 Set the arguments of the OpenCL kernel

```
1   int setKernelArgs() {
2       cl_int status;
3       status = clSetKernelArg(kernel, 0, sizeof(cl_mem), &d_A);
4       status |= clSetKernelArg(kernel, 1, sizeof(cl_mem), &d_B);
5       status |= clSetKernelArg(kernel, 2, sizeof(cl_mem), &d_C);
6       status |= clSetKernelArg(kernel, 3, sizeof(cl_int), &elements1D);
7       status |= clSetKernelArg(kernel, 4, sizeof(cl_int), &elements1D);
8       status |= clSetKernelArg(kernel, 5, sizeof(cl_int), &elements1D);
9
10      if (CL_SUCCESS != status) {
11          cout << "Error in clSetKernelArg, status: " << status << endl;
12      }
13      return status;
14  }
```

Step 4. Launch the Execution of the Kernel Object

This step is responsible for launching the execution of the created kernel object. Listing 3.8 presents the function that launches the matrix multiplication kernel for execution on the GPU device. Lines 2–9 define the global and local work group size as have been described in Sect. 3.4.3. The OpenCL command that offloads the kernel for execution with the configured global work group size is listed in lines 11–12.

Listing 3.8 Launch of the OpenCL kernel

```
1   int launchKernel() {
2       size_t globalWorkSize[2];
3       size_t localWorkSize[3];
4
5       globalWorkSize[0] = elements1D;
6       globalWorkSize[1] = elements1D;
7       localWorkSize[0] = LOCAL_WORK_SIZE;
8       localWorkSize[1] = 1;
9       localWorkSize[2] = 1;
10
11      return clEnqueueNDRangeKernel(commandQueue, kernel, 2, NULL,
12              globalWorkSize, localWorkSize, 0, NULL, &kernelEvent);
13  }
```

Step 5. Transfer Result Data from Device to Host

Finally, this step performs the transferring of the result data from device to host. Listing 3.9 presents the OpenCL command that reads the result data of matrix C from the global memory of the GPU device to the address space that is pointed by array C. Line 4 flushes the enqueued commands that reside in the command queue to be issued to the device.

Listing 3.9 OpenCL command for transferring result data from device to host

```
1  void transferResultDataFromPlatform() {
2      clEnqueueReadBuffer(commandQueue, d_C, CL_TRUE, 0, datasize, C,
3                  0, NULL, &readEvent);
4      clFlush(commandQueue);
5  }
```

3.5.2   An Example of a CUDA Program

The CUDA implementation of matrix multiplication comprises both the host code and the device code in a single program file (i.e., namely host.cu); a property known as single-source development. The CUDA function is a parallel implementation of matrix multiplication and is presented in Listing 3.10. Lines 1–2 show the declaration of the kernel, while the remaining lines represent the kernel body. The CUDA function shown in Listing 3.10 is functionally equivalent with the OpenCL kernel that we showed in the previous section (Listing 3.2). Thus, the CUDA kernel also replaces the indices of the two outermost loops with the thread identifiers that correspond to the two grid dimensions, as shown in lines 3–4.

Listing 3.10 OpenCL C kernel for matrix multiplication

```
1  __global__ void matrix_multiplication(float *a, float *b, float *c,
2          int sizeX, int sizeY, int width) {
3      int i = blockIdx.x * blockDim.x + threadIdx.x;
4      int j = blockIdx.y * blockDim.y + threadIdx.y;
5
6      if (i < sizeX && j < sizeY) {
7          float sum = 0.0f;
8          for (int k = 0; k < width; k++) {
9              sum += a[k * sizeX + i] * b[j * width + k];
10         }
11         c[j * sizeX + i] = sum;
12     }
13 }
```

Similar to the OpenCL program that we discussed in the previous section, the host code of the CUDA program also contains some auxiliary tasks and some primary tasks. The auxiliary tasks contain mainly the initialization of the input data and the validation of the result data from the GPU. The primary tasks correspond to the material discussed in this chapter and they are executed in four steps, as follows:

1. Initialize the CUDA events and the necessary data buffers, as discussed in Sect. 3.4.1.
2. Transfer input data from host to device, as explained in Sect. 3.4.2.
3. Launch the execution of the CUDA function.
4. Transfer result data from device to host, as explained in Sect. 3.4.4.

Our CUDA implementation has one task less than the OpenCL implementation which has been described in Sect. 3.5.1. The reason is that we have used the CUDA Runtime API which is less verbose than the CUDA Driver API, the OpenCL Runtime API, and the Intel oneAPI Level Zero API (see Sect. 3.4.1). The CUDA Runtime API does not require programmers to explicitly create data structures and set the kernel arguments before launching the kernel. In contrast, it enables programmers to directly invoke the kernel function with the appropriate grid and block dimensions, as will be discussed later in Action 3 and is shown in Listing 3.14.

If programmers wish to customize or explicitly create low-level CUDA data structures, such as CUDA streams, CUDA modules or the kernel objects (also known as cudaFunction_t in CUDA), they can use the CUDA Driver API.

Step 1. Initialize the CUDA Events and Data Buffers

The first step is to create and define the CUDA events which are related to particular kernel operations (e.g., data transfers, kernel execution) and the necessary data buffers. Listing 3.11 presents the creation of six CUDA events, which include two events for the three kernel operations (i.e., transferring input data, kernel execution, transferring result data). Listing 3.12 shows the creation of three CUDA data buffers in lines 2-4, via the cudaMalloc function.

Listing 3.11 Initialization of CUDA events

```
1  void initializeCUDAEvents() {
2      cudaEventCreate(&startWriteEvent);
3      cudaEventCreate(&stopWriteEvent);
4      cudaEventCreate(&startKernelEvent);
5      cudaEventCreate(&stopKernelEvent);
6      cudaEventCreate(&startReadEvent);
7      cudaEventCreate(&stopReadEvent);
8  }
```

Listing 3.12 Creation of CUDA data buffers

```
1  void createDataBuffers() {
2      cudaMalloc(&d_A, datasize);
3      cudaMalloc(&d_B, datasize);
4      cudaMalloc(&d_C, datasize);
5  }
```

Step 2. Transfer Input Data from Host to Device

The second step concerns the transferring of input data from host to device. Listing 3.13 shows in lines 3–10 the CUDA commands that copy the input data of matrices A_seq and B_seq to the area that has been allocated in the global memory of the GPU device.

Listing 3.13 CUDA Commands for transferring input data from host to device

```
1   void transferInputDataToPlatform() {
2       cudaError_t status;
3       status = cudaMemcpy(d_A, A_seq, datasize, cudaMemcpyHostToDevice);
4       if (status != cudaSuccess) {
5           cout << "Error in cudaMemcpy for array d_A, status: " << status << endl;
6       }
7       status = cudaMemcpy(d_B, B_seq, datasize, cudaMemcpyHostToDevice);
8       if (status != cudaSuccess) {
9           cout << "Error in cudaMemcpy for array d_B, status: " << status << endl;
10      }
11  }
```

Step 3. Launch the Execution of the Kernel Object

This step is responsible for launching the execution of the created kernel object. Listing 3.14 presents the function that launches the matrix multiplication kernel for execution on the GPU device. Lines 2–3 define the grid and block dimensions, which correspond to the global and local work group size. The CUDA command that offloads the kernel for execution with the configured block and grid dimension is listed in lines 9–10. Line 11 presents a blocking call that awaits the completion of the kernel execution.

Listing 3.14 Launching of the CUDA kernel

```
1   void launchKernel() {
2       dim3 grimDim(elements1D, elements1D);
3       dim3 blockDimPerGrid(1, 1);
4       if (numOfElements > elements1D){
5           blockDimPerGrid.x = ceil(double(elements1D)/double(grimDim.x));
6           blockDimPerGrid.y = ceil(double(elements1D)/double(grimDim.y));
7       }
```

```
 8
 9      matrix_multiplication<<<grimDim,blockDimPerGrid>>>(d_A, d_B, d_C,
10          elements1D, elements1D, width);
11      cudaDeviceSynchronize();
12  }
```

Step 4. Transfer Result Data from Device to Host

Finally, this step performs the transferring of the result data from device to host. Listing 3.15 presents the CUDA command that copies the result data from the allocated area (d_C) in the global memory of the GPU device to the address space that is pointed by array C. Line 6 performs a blocking call until the result data has been copied to array C.

Listing 3.15 CUDA command for transferring result data from device to host

```
1  void transferResultDataFromPlatform() {
2      cudaError_t status = cudaMemcpy(C, d_C, datasize, cudaMemcpyDeviceToHost);
3      if (status != cudaSuccess) {
4          cout << "Error in cudaMemcpy for array d_C, status: " << status << endl;
5      }
6      cudaDeviceSynchronize();
7  }
```

3.6 Summary

This chapter introduced readers to the programming models for heterogeneous hardware devices, and demonstrated how they can be used by programmers. At first, it gave the definition of a programming model and outlined the state-of-the-art programming models that have been vastly used in a large range of the software market. Then, this chapter presented the basic building blocks of heterogeneous programming models. To narrow down the scope and assist readers, this book has focused on OpenCL which is considered as forerunner of several recent programming models. Finally, it demonstrated examples of how OpenCL and CUDA programs written in C++ can use the building blocks of the employed programming models in order to offload part of their code segments to run on a hardware accelerator device. Readers will find supplementary exercises to reflect on the material discussed in this Chap. [15].

The next chapter will introduce the managed runtime environments which execute managed programming languages, such as Java, JavaScript, Python, etc. Furthermore, it will explain the challenges posed by the heterogeneous programming models for hardware acceleration, that were discussed in this chapter, to managed runtime environments.

Chapter 4
Managed Runtime Environments

4.1 Introduction on MREs

A Managed Runtime Environment is a virtual execution environment that lies in between the hardware and the user level code, as shown in Fig. 4.1. An MRE is also referred to as a Virtual Machine (VM); hence, the term JVM for the Java Virtual Machine. The purpose of the MRE is to abstract away the low level hardware details from the developers while, in parallel, enabling features such as dynamic compilation, automatic memory management, and others. Both in industry and in academia numerous MREs exist that support different programming languages [24–26]. Additionally, different implementations of MREs for the same programming language can be found [24, 49].

Typically, dynamic programming languages require the presence of an MRE in order to execute user programs. However, there are cases where although the users write their programs in a dynamic programming language, underlying technologies can create a static ahead-of-time binary executable that can run directly; without requiring the presence of an MRE [31]. In this book, we will not delve into statically compiled binaries of dynamic programming languages but we will rather focus on the dynamic execution of programs written in said languages. The reason behind that is that this book attempts to shed light and explain the challenges that hardware acceleration brings into MREs, rather than trying to list all possible execution scenarios of all programming languages via the various and diverse underlying execution systems.

Relationship between MREs and Dynamic Programming Languages
As already mentioned, dynamic programming languages such as Java, Python, etc., are typically designed around a language specification which is honored by the underlying MRE upon which they execute. Hence, it is expected that at least one implementation of an MRE exists for a dynamic language. Additionally, MREs have evolved over the years and we can now find implementations of multiple

© The Author(s), under exclusive license to Springer Nature Switzerland AG 2024
J. Fumero et al., *Programming Heterogeneous Hardware via Managed Runtime Systems*, SpringerBriefs in Computer Science,
https://doi.org/10.1007/978-3-031-49559-5_4

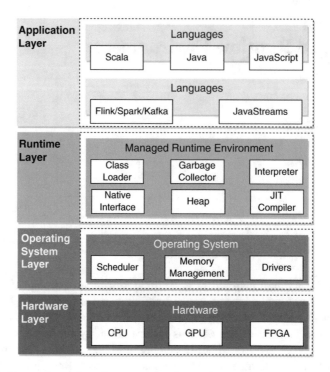

Fig. 4.1 Architectural overview of a managed runtime environment

programming languages running on top of the same MRE (e.g., JRuby [32] and Truffle-based languages [40] that run on top of the JVM). Regardless of the relationship between a programming language and the underlying MRE, the core components of MREs are commonly found amongst different implementations. Consequently, when trying to combine these components with heterogeneous programming models, a number of challenges arise, as it will be discussed in the later sections. Before we discuss those challenges, we first need to gain an overview knowledge of the core components of MREs.

4.2   Core Components

Figure 4.2 provides a depiction of the internal architecture of an abstract MRE, inspired by the Java Virtual Machine which is the most commonly used MRE.

As shown in Fig. 4.2, an MRE consists broadly of five key components:

1. Interpreter
2. Just-In-Time (JIT) compiler(s)
3. Memory Heap and Garbage Collector(s)

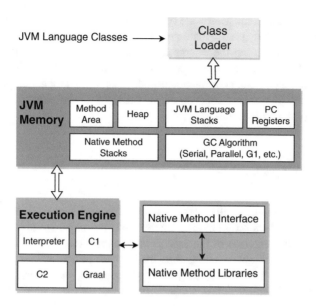

Fig. 4.2 Core components of an MRE, inspired by the JVM

4. Native substrate
5. Class loader(s)

All those components work in collaboration to essentially enable the dynamic execution of a programming language. The typical execution flow of the user code is as follows:

- Users write their program in a programming language of choice.
- (Optionally) a first static compilation transforms the user program into an intermediate representation (e.g., Java bytecodes).
- The intermediate bytecodes are consequently executed on top of the MRE via means of interpretation or JIT compilation in various forms.

To make the abstract execution flow above more concrete, we use the example of the Java programming language:

- Users write their programs in Java or any other programming language that can be executed on top of the JVM (e.g., Kotlin, Ruby, etc.).
- The resulted source code is compiled by `javac` to produce *class* files that contain all generated bytecodes.
- The class files are then passed to the MRE (`java` command), which loads them and executes them via the included interpreters or the different JIT compilers included in the particular JVM distribution (e.g., in OpenJDK the C1, C2, or Graal compilers).

As explained above, the MREs are typically involved during the execution of the bytecodes or any other intermediate representation. The machine code generation occurs dynamically during the interpretation or JIT compilation of the bytecodes. We elaborate further into the compilation process in Sect. 4.3 since it is one of the key factors influencing the heterogeneous code execution of managed programming languages. The remainder of this subsection provides a brief description of the key components typically found in MREs.

4.2.1 Class Loader

Upon launching execution, the Class Loader subsystem that loads and parses the .class files of a Java program is being invoked. The objective of the class loader is to create a representation of the loaded classes (and soon to be executed within the Java Virtual Machine), which is then loaded onto memory. This representation regards the classes themselves, their methods, and any variables. In addition, a typical JVM has multiple class loaders which are invoked hierarchically (e.g., Bootstrap, Extension, and Application class loaders). Following class loading, the JVM-internal objects that represent the loaded classes are initialized along with their static variables and stored in the heap; a memory area that is explained in Sect. 4.2.3.

4.2.2 Interpreter/JIT Compilers

After the Java classes have been loaded onto memory and their bytecodes are accessible by the JVM, execution can commence. Bytecode execution is typically performed by—what we call—the *execution engine* of the JVM which can potentially contain a bytecode interpreter and a number of JIT compilers of different capabilities.

Initially, the Java bytecode interpreter drives the execution by parsing the bytecodes—typically one at a time—and translating them into machine code compatible with the underlying architecture that the JVM is executing on. Bytecode interpretation can start immediately after class loading, and hence, minimize the latency between bootstrapping the JVM and starting execution. However, since no compilation and no forms of optimizations are applied, the performance of interpreters is typically much lower to that of JIT-compiled methods [80].

The JVM, and almost all MREs, address the slow interpretation times by incorporating a number of JIT compilers that are being invoked when *hot methods* are encountered. A hot method is a method which is being frequently invoked by the executed program. Hence, it is deemed worthy to spend the compilation time in order to produce an optimized version of that method at the assembly level. Typically, the interpreters profile the executed code by recording the invocation counts of methods. Based on a threshold defined by the JIT compiler, when a method

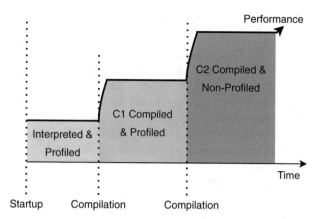

Fig. 4.3 Tiered compilation in the JVM

invocation count surpasses a predefined number then it is being compiled by the JIT compiler; synchronously or asynchronously. When the compilation finishes, the generated machine code of the method is being installed in the code cache and any subsequent invocation of this method will execute the optimized code.

Throughout the years, the performance of JIT compilers (in terms of produced code quality) has been increased dramatically by the use of more aggressive and speculative compiler optimizations [42]. Typically, the more optimizations a compiler performs, the longer the compilation time is. To address potentially long compilation times, modern MREs follow a tiered-compilation approach (Fig. 4.3) in which different compilers with different optimization capabilities are being gradually invoked. For example, OpenJDK provides three distinct JIT compilers for the JVM; namely, C1, C2, and Graal. Each compiler contains different optimizations, with Graal being the most aggressive and highest performing on average. On the other hand, C1 (also referred to as the client compiler) produces less optimal code than Graal, but its compilation times are lower. Finally, C2 falls in-between the two previous compilers, but it is closer to the characteristics of Graal.

The high quality, and hence the high performance, of the machine code produced by dynamic JIT compilers is achieved via speculation (in some cases). This means that the compiler will speculate upon the behavior of a method, and hence perform optimizations based on that speculation. For example, if the profiling data indicate that a specific code path is never executed, the optimizing compiler may decide to remove this execution path and instead add an assertion. If during execution, execution is steered to the removed code section, the assertion will be triggered and the *de-optimization* process of the JVM will be triggered. This process will restore the state of the JVM at the necessary execution point (where the failure occurred) and will resume execution with the interpreter. Consequently, the optimized machine code will be discarded and a new version will be re-created with the new profiling data following the optimization process described above.

4.2.3   Memory Allocation and GC

The automatic memory management subsystem of an MRE is a key part of the execution of applications since it abstracts away the need for explicit memory allocation and management from developers. This subsystem typically has two components: (a) the memory allocator, and (b) the Garbage Collector (GC). There has been significant research over the last 40 years in techniques and algorithms for optimizing GC and memory allocation policies within MREs [44] and current state-of-the-art production MREs provide a plethora of choices regarding GC algorithms and allocation policies.

Typically, an application running on top of an MRE, allocates objects in a managed memory area created by the MRE which is called the heap. Application threads use specific keywords from the language-provided APIs and the underlying MREs allocate memory which is then initialized with the correct values (e.g., new keyword in Java). To avoid contention over the shared application heap, threads typically allocate objects within thread local allocation buffers (or TLABs) via bump pointer allocation policies. When a TLAB of a particular thread is full, the MRE requests a new one from the memory allocator following proper synchronization policies to avoid race conditions amongst threads. Although the majority of the objects are typically allocated in the application heap, MREs provide also capabilities to allocate data outside the heap; implicitly or explicitly. If for example, an application has a large dataset which is global and persistent across the whole execution, it makes sense to allocate it off-heap in order to save time from the GC checking whether the data of this dataset are still being used (e.g., Neo4J page cache[1]).

When the application heap is full, the GC is being called in order to free memory. There are numerous GC algorithms, techniques, and approaches to achieve this objective. In addition, different GC algorithms have different optimization objectives; e.g., optimize latency versus throughput. Hence, different applications that have different requirements may utilize different GC. This is the reason that modern MREs utilize a number of GCs with different optimization parameters that users can select (e.g., OpenJDK Parallel, G1, ZGC, Shenandoah GCs).

Regardless of the GC type, from a high level point of view their operational objectives are identical. When operating, the GC tries to find *live* objects; i.e., objects that are still referenced by the stack, registers, or other places in the MRE. Upon creating the transitive closure of all live objects, the remaining are considered *dead* and therefore the memory they occupy can be reclaimed. Both live object discovery and memory reclamation can take many forms; e.g., Tracing, Reference Counting, Copying/Evacuation, Compaction, etc. GCs typically run in cycles, and they keep freeing memory for the MRE on-demand. In some cases GCs pose performance challenges to applications since they work concurrently with the

---

[1] https://neo4j.com/developer/guide-performance-tuning.

application threads (concurrent GCs) or they may stop the application threads (Stop-The-World GCs) to perform some operations. The performance implications of GCs have been an active topic of research both at the industrial and academic levels with constant innovations being delivered generation-after-generation.

4.2.4   Interfacing with Native Code

It is quite common for MREs to communicate with native functions or system libraries. Hence, specific functionalities are supplied via MREs to enable programming languages executed on top of them, to access such native code. Usually, these transitions are slow since extra work is required to achieve downward and upward calls (from the managed world to the native one, and vice versa). For example, the JVM supports this functionality via the Java Native Interface (JNI) which poses some overheads mainly due to auxiliary activities that have to be done such as wrapping/unwrapping arguments and results, matching different calling conventions for native and Java code, etc. Fast native calls are of great importance when enabling heterogeneous hardware execution of MREs since frequent communication must be established with the native runtime layer of the underlying programming interfaces such as OpenCL and CUDA. To that end, new initiatives such as OpenJDK Project Panama [83] or Alibaba's FFI [84] have been developed to increase the performance of native calls.

4.3   Challenges of Heterogeneous Code Execution via MREs

From their initial conception, MREs have been designed and built around the "write-once-run-everywhere" paradigm. The idea is that instead of building ahead of time architecture-dependent binaries for execution, developers write their applications once and then they can deploy them across different architectures seamlessly. This is achieved by the use of an MRE which abstracts away the low-level hardware details from developers. Architecture-dependent tasks such as machine code generation, memory management, and others are handled by the MRE and the system developers of those MREs are responsible for augmenting the systems to support multiple hardware architectures.

Unfortunately, these design decisions that enable the "write-once-run-everywhere" approach of MREs, are the same ones that pose significant challenges when it comes to heterogeneous hardware acceleration. These challenges stem from two major facts: (1) MREs have been initially designed to target only CPUs with different ISAs (Instruction Set Architectures), and (2) hardware accelerators are quite different from CPUs both in terms of capabilities and execution models. Hence, in order to transition MREs into this heterogeneous world, numerous changes are necessitated at the system level.

Fig. 4.4 Typical
heterogeneous execution
workflow

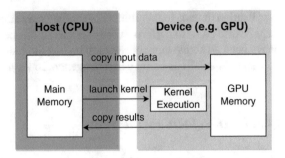

After having introduced the core components of MREs (Sect. 4.2) along with
the fundamentals of heterogeneous programming models (Chap. 3), it is time to
explore how these two worlds can converge and what challenges MREs pose in
this endeavor.

4.3.1 Heterogeneous Execution Workflow

As explained in Sect. 3, a typical heterogeneous execution workflow entails the
three actions illustrated in Fig. 4.4. As shown in Fig. 4.4, the three distinct steps
of heterogeneous code execution are:

1. Copy data from the host's memory (typically a CPU) to the accelerators' memory
   (e.g., a GPU).
2. Process the data on the accelerator.
3. Copy the results of the execution from the accelerator's memory back to the host
   memory.

Having this typical heterogeneous execution flow in mind, in the next sections
we will elaborate further on how some components of MREs pose challenges to
this execution flow. The following sections recap the main components of MREs
by adding extra information which is required to expand on the challenges of
heterogeneous execution.

4.3.2 Code Generation

As explained in Sect. 4.2.2, MREs follow a tiered-compilation approach starting
code execution via interpretation and progressively produce more optimized code
via JIT compilation when *hot* methods are discovered. Compilation in MREs takes
place at the method level and different implementations include different compilers
that employ different Intermediate Representation (IR) [41] types; with the most
common being the Single Static Assignment (SSA) [41] form. When the compiler

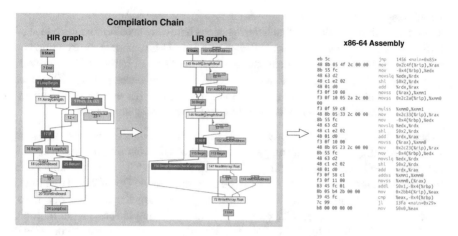

Fig. 4.5 A typical compilation chain

is being invoked to compile a method, the method's bytecodes are being parsed and the IR of the method is being created. Typically, each compiler has its own IR implementation.

Consequently, numerous optimizations are being applied to the IR graph which is progressively "lowered" from its High form to its Low form; hence the nomenclature found in compilers HIR (High-level IR) and LIR (Low-level IR). Depending on the level of the IR during compilation, different types of optimizations are applied. In addition, as the IR is being "lowered" from its High presentation to the Lower one, more architectural-specific information is being introduced to it. Finally, at the final stages of compilation, the machine code is generated, the code is being installed in the code cache, and any consequent calls to this method will invoke the optimized machine code. Figure 4.5, exemplifies the compilation chain of a method by showcasing the transition from HIR to LIR and finally to assembly generation.

As explained above, the transition between HIR to LIR gradually exposes (in the IR) the various architectural characteristics of the underlying hardware platform. For example, if JIT compilation occurs on a x86 system, then the architectural characteristics such as addressing modes, registers, etc., are introduced to the IR. Likewise, if the target architecture is ARM or any other, the same process occurs. A common denominator, regardless of the underlying architecture, is that MREs have been designed to primarily target CPUs rather than hardware accelerators. As explained in Chap. 2, heterogeneous hardware accelerators are substantially different to CPUs since they have been designed for executing certain workloads with specific characteristics. For example, GPUs are designed for high-throughput parallel workloads. These architectural differences pose a number of challenges to the compilation chains that current modern MREs employ.

Challenges

To understand the challenges that heterogeneous hardware accelerators introduce on the compilation chains of modern MREs, we will use as an example the execution on GPUs. Broadly, the same challenges apply to other types of hardware accelerators. Regarding code generation for heterogeneous hardware accelerators, MREs face two main challenges: (1) machine code generation, and (2) exposure of domain-specific programming constructs to high level programming languages.

Machine Code Generation As explained in Sect. 3, heterogeneous hardware accelerators are typically accompanied by dedicated programming models. For example, GPUs can be programmed via CUDA, OpenCL, oneAPI and other programming models, while FPGAs can be programmed via OpenCL or High Level Synthesis (HLS) tools. A number of those tools can target more than one hardware accelerator (e.g., OpenCL, oneAPI support multiple platforms from multiple vendors), while others (e.g., CUDA) support only a particular device type (GPU) from one vendor (NVIDIA). Table 3.1 provided an overview of said programming models and the devices they support. The aforementioned programming models are optimized for their underlying platforms via their compilation chains and driver implementations. In order for an MRE to target a hardware accelerator (e.g., GPU), it must extends its compilation chain to generate code that is compatible with these underlying heterogeneous programming models.

In other words, there must be a way that during JIT compilation, instead of generating binary instructions supported by a CPU, the MRE has to generate code that can be supplied to the heterogeneous programming model that resides underneath the MRE. For example, the MRE must add support for generating PTX instructions that target CUDA, or SPIR-V which can be used via OpenCL or Intel's Level Zero. Extending a compiler and its IR to generate such instructions, however, is not a trivial task since the target instructions differ significantly compared to the standard CPU oriented IR. For example programming models such as CUDA and OpenCL expose to developers parallel constructs such as thread dimensions, barriers, etc., that somehow must be integrated into the existing compilation chains. Therefore, abstracting away such architectural details via an MRE is more complicated in the case of heterogeneous accelerators due to the incompatibility between the current programming languages (and their existing compilation chains) and the more specific programming models that are being used in hardware accelerators. Chapter 5 explains the state-of-the-art solutions that currently exist for generating heterogeneous code via MREs.

Domain-Specific Constructs The architectural characteristics of a heterogeneous hardware accelerator (described in Chap. 2), and their exposure to the compilation chain of current MREs create specific challenges that necessitate the expansion of the IR to incorporate such constructs. In addition, these changes might be also accompanied with extensions to the programming model of the programming language exposed to the developers. For example, in the case of GPUs, developers must explicitly define the parallelism of the applications by using dimensional

grids (from 1D to 3D), as explained in Sect. 3. Developers define the workload
of each thread and during the execution on a GPU, a large number of threads are
spawned and mapped to the dimensional grid; and each one of those threads execute
their part of the computation. In addition, constructs for defining synchronization
points between threads in the form of barriers, or constructs for defining types
of memory used on the GPU such as local or global memory, are essential for
GPU programming. These constructs must be used by the MRE either explicitly
or implicitly (or both). Chapter 5, explains how modern solutions for enabling
heterogeneous hardware acceleration on MREs address these challenges.

4.3.3 Runtime Support

In this book, the term "runtime support" in MREs is defined as the underlying
native components that an MRE requires in order to execute. For example, methods
for allocating native memory, or the machinery to map Java threads to native OS-
level pthreads are part of what we define here as "runtime support". As we
already explained above, in order for an MRE to execute code on a heterogeneous
hardware accelerator, it must utilize (in some way or form), the programming model
supported by the particular accelerator (e.g., CUDA or OpenCL). The presence
of those heterogeneous programming models and their integration with MREs,
essentially creates two worlds that must communicate and work in harmony to
enable heterogeneous execution. Consequently, part of that harmonic execution
is the cooperation at the runtime level. For example, functionalities that enable
memory allocation and memory management on a GPU are part of the runtime layer
of CUDA or OpenCL and must be integrated within the MRE. That integration poses
a number of challenges mainly due to transitions between the "managed world" and
the native functions of the integrated underlying runtime layers.

Challenges
In practical terms, integrating a heterogeneous programming model (e.g., OpenCL
or CUDA) with an MRE requires the implementation of "glue code" between
the MRE and these programming models. The glue code essentially bridges the
functionalities necessitated by the MRE and their implementation in OpenCL or
CUDA. An example that demonstrates such integration is the memory allocation.
In order to allocate memory on a GPU, specific native system calls provided by
OpenCL or CUDA must be invoked. When we try to execute user code atop of an
MRE (e.g., Java or Python) that is prime for hardware acceleration, the underlying
runtime implementation must allocate memory on the GPU, and copy the data
from the MRE world to the hardware accelerator. There are many variations of this
execution flow but for simplicity we explain the common scenario. The runtime
support to accompany this execution flow must be implemented at the MRE level
and be invoked either implicitly (by the MRE) or explicitly (by the developers

via an explicit native call). The current solutions for adding runtime support for heterogeneous programming within MREs are explained in Chap. 5.

4.3.4   Memory Management

As already mentioned in Sect. 4.2.3, automatic memory management is one of the key pillars of MREs. Instead of manually allocating memory as in native languages such as C and C++, the MRE performs both the allocation and the memory management completely transparently to developers. Typically, MREs allocate their data into a dedicated memory area called "heap". Depending on the memory allocation policy and Garbage Collection algorithm(s) of the MREs, the heap can be allocated in a contiguous memory address space or divided across various memory spaces that comprise the heap altogether. Memory allocation techniques and GC algorithms have been an active research area which unfortunately can not be covered in the context of this book. For detailed analysis on such topics please refer to the excellent memory management book by Jones et al. [44]. Regardless of which memory allocation policy or GC algorithm a particular MRE uses, in the context of heterogeneous execution, the challenges are orthogonal and they mainly derive from the fact that—in most cases—a host device (e.g., CPU) and a hardware accelerator (e.g., GPU) have distinct physical memories.

Challenges
In a typical heterogeneous system, a host CPU is connected via an interconnect (e.g., PCIe) to external hardware devices that serve the role of hardware accelerators. In addition, modern CPUs in the form of System-On-Chips (SOCs) integrate several accelerators such as integrated GPUs (iGPUs), vector units, crypto modules, AI/ML accelerators and others. In the latter case, where the accelerators are within the SoC, they share the physical memory with the CPU. In the former case, where the accelerators are external to the CPU, they use their own physical memory (e.g., a discrete GPU—dGPU). Modern MREs have been designed for CPU-only execution and hence their automatic memory management regards a single physical memory which is coherent across threads. Memory consistency across threads is guaranteed by the developers via the usage of thread-safe data structures or memory synchronization primitives such as locks, semaphores, and monitors. When we extend an MRE to account for hardware accelerators, the assumptions upon which MREs have designed the memory allocators and GC algorithms do not hold true anymore. In the case of discrete hardware accelerators, a separate physical memory is being added to the total execution which is not visible to the GC. Hence the GC must be extended to also perform operations on this discrete physical memory. This requires changes to the driver implementation of the underlying heterogeneous programming model (e.g., OpenCL or CUDA) to keep track of objects or data present on the accelerator's memory. Even in the case of integrated hardware accelerators where the separate physical memory is not an issue, controlling

execution of threads and tracking memory references is still a significant challenge. In a typical CPU-only scenario, when memory becomes full, a GC is being invoked to reclaim memory space from "dead" objects. To achieve that, specific safepoints are being polled in order for the application threads to stop executing, allowing the GC to reclaim memory and update the memory references. This process is typically found in stop-the-world (STW) GCs, while in modern concurrent GC, application and GC threads work concurrently with memory consistency being possible with the usage of read and write barriers [44]. Regardless of the type of GC (STW or concurrent), when executing on a hardware accelerator, the implementation of those mechanisms is very expensive in terms of performance. For example, any control flow in the code generated for a GPU has a significant performance overhead, mainly due to the lack of hardware branch predictors in GPUs (Chap. 2). In addition, GPUs have been designed for accelerating highly data parallel workloads with minimum to zero control flow divergence.

4.3.5 Performance Considerations

Another important factor to consider when adding heterogeneous hardware support to MREs is that of performance. Although performance considerations are orthogonal to programming languages—whether they are dynamic and use an MRE or not—MREs add additional challenges. In general, in order to benefit from heterogeneous hardware acceleration a number of conditions must be satisfied:

- **Workload suitability:** Each hardware accelerator is suitable for a particular workload type (Chap. 2). For example, GPUs are better for highly parallel workload and FPGAs are suitable for pipeline parallelism. Hence, when considering hardware acceleration for a particular workload or use, careful consideration must be given to understand which parts of the code exhibit characteristics that are suitable for a specific hardware accelerator. If we try to run on an accelerator a workload that is not tailored for it, then we will certainly encounter performance degradations compared to CPU execution. For example, trying to execute a workload with significant control flow divergence on a GPU.
- **Data movement overheads:** Discrete hardware accelerators typically have their own physical memories and hence data has to be copied from the hosts' memories to the accelerators' memories. In addition, when the accelerator finishes its execution, the results must be also copied back from the accelerator to the hosts' memory. The overheads of those data copies must be offset by the performance gains of the hardware acceleration in order for the performance benefits to be visible to the end-users.
- **Use-case specific requirements:** Some applications may have specific requirements that might be affected or invalidated by the hardware acceleration. For example, applications that rely on streaming data to perform real time operations might not benefit from hardware acceleration on devices that require bulk data to

perform batch processing (e.g., GPUs). In addition, other requirements such as latency, power consumption, or other might be negatively affected by hardware acceleration.

Despite the aforementioned general conditions for achieving benefits from hardware acceleration, MREs pose additional ones that we have to consider.

Challenges
Regarding performance, the most significant differentiating factor of MREs compared to native languages is the implications of the GC. When executing parts of an application on a hardware accelerator, the GC does not have a view of the data generated or altered on the device (e.g., GPU). Hence, the parts of the applications that execute on the host (e.g., CPU) must not access the data that reside in the device memory since this can cause stale references or values. Similarly, the GC shall not move data that reside in the device's memory. To solve those issues, typically the GC is blocked when syncing data between the host and the device. Blocking the GC may impose performance degradations across the whole running application since it will have collateral effects across the whole system and its performance. Another performance consideration, in the context of MREs, is the costly numerous transitions between the managed world and the native world. As already mentioned, in order to execute code on a hardware accelerator, special runtime support is required to bridge the two worlds (the managed world of the MRE and the native world of the heterogeneous programming frameworks; e.g., CUDA or OpenCL). Utilizing that runtime support, entails the execution of numerous function calls that transition between the managed and the native systems (e.g., Java Native Interface calls in the JVM). Those expensive calls reduce the overall end-to-end performance of the system and, hence, special consideration shall be given to minimize them in order to ameliorate their negative effects on performance.

4.4   Summary

This chapter provided a brief introduction on how MREs operate by outlining their key architectural components and their interoperability. After providing the foundational knowledge on MREs, this chapter elaborated on the challenges that heterogeneous programming models pose to MREs when trying to integrate them together. Namely, the challenges of heterogeneous execution on code generation, runtime support, memory management, and performance have been discussed. The discussion on those challenges aims to shed light into the complexities of expanding the scope of MREs towards incorporating heterogeneous hardware accelerators into their execution models. Understanding those challenges is vital in order to comprehend and appreciate the current state-of-the-art solutions for heterogeneous acceleration of MREs described in the following chapter. Readers will find supplementary exercises to reflect on the material discussed in this chapter [16].

Chapter 5
Programming Heterogeneous Hardware via Managed Runtime Systems

5.1 Overview of Current Approaches

The last chapter described the challenges posed by programming hardware accelerators from managed programming languages, such as Java, C#, Python, or JavaScript. Those challenges have been attributed to the differences in memory management, concurrency models, and the need to interface with native code for utilizing the heterogeneous programming models. To that end, many approaches have been identified to address the aforementioned challenges and bridge that gap between hardware acceleration and managed languages.

In this chapter, we separate the approaches into three categories: (1) programming wrapper interfaces that expose low-level information of heterogeneous programming models to managed languages (Sect. 5.2); (2) software libraries that expose APIs that implicitly use static predefined functions that can run on hardware accelerators; The functions are referred hereafter as prebuilt functions (Sect. 5.3); and (3) parallel programming frameworks that employ JIT compilation to handle compilation of user defined functions (UDFs), data manipulation and GPU kernel dispatching in a transparent manner (Sect. 5.4). For each category, we describe the pros and cons and present code snippets of examples implemented in various programming frameworks.

In particular, we opt to examine programming frameworks in the scope of Java and Python; as they are both programming languages that run on top of an MRE. Thus, we focus on the most common programming frameworks for heterogeneous hardware accelerators, such as ArrayFire, PyTorch, JOCL and TornadoVM. Note that some programming frameworks being explained in this chapter are in production, while others are research projects. However, they are mature enough to be reproduced in many programming environments and operating systems, and they help to illustrate the challenges and solutions that each of the frameworks provide. Additionally, this chapter demonstrates code snippets of using

J. Fumero et al., *Programming Heterogeneous Hardware via Managed Runtime Systems*, SpringerBriefs in Computer Science, https://doi.org/10.1007/978-3-031-49559-5_5

those programming frameworks and highlights the pros and cons of each approach. All the code examples presented in this chapter are available in GitHub as open-source software [59].

Upon completion of this chapter, the reader should be aware of how to program hardware accelerators (and in particular GPUs) from managed programming languages. Therefore, Sect. 5.6 summarizes the key points of this chapter.

> Although this chapter discusses specifically Java and Python as the examined programming languages, all approaches presented in this chapter can be transferable, or already exist, in other managed runtime environments. For example, there are programming frameworks (e.g., Dandelion [58]) that employ hardware acceleration on GPUs and FPGAs for the Microsoft .NET Framework.

5.2   Programming with Wrapper Interfaces

One possible way to program heterogeneous hardware from managed runtime environments is via wrapper interfaces. We define a wrapper interface as an interface that enables high level programming languages to offload execution of a program on a hardware accelerator. In practice, developers must define the computation to be offloaded on an accelerator in the form of a kernel function written in OpenCL C, CUDA, etc. The kernel function is stored in a `string` type which is consumed by the wrapper interface. For example, developers can execute an OpenCL kernel from a Java program by providing the OpenCL C kernel as a Java string.

Besides the usage of kernel functions, a wrapper interface also exposes to managed languages a group of native functions responsible for the orchestration of the execution. In essence, those functions implement the kernels (e.g., GPU kernels) of the low-level accelerators' programming models (see Sect. 3.4), and the user program is used as a proxy application that invokes the kernels and handler for memory and execution. To do so, developers directly invoke native code (usually code written in C/C/++) from high-level programming languages to communicate with the corresponding drivers (e.g., OpenCL runtime). This is because standards such as OpenCL and SYCL, or heterogeneous parallel programming models such as CUDA, are defined and implemented for C and C++. Thus, in order to dispatch and interact with the heterogeneous hardware, programmers using high-level programming languages, need to invoke native code.

Although the engineering of wrapper interfaces which expose native functionality to an MRE is a common practice to expose library interoperability in cross-language and runtime environments, such as the Java Native Interface (JNI) [97], it is not ideal due to the complexity and the high cost of maintenance. However, possible syntax errors cannot be caught at compile time from the user program (e.g., Java program), but rather at runtime, when the kernel functions are compiled by the accelerators' drivers. But this approach allows developers to have access to non-standard and low-level libraries quicker compared to other approaches, offering high-level of control and fast access to accelerators.

To present an overview of a wrapper interface and show how to use it to access hardware accelerators, we have structured the next paragraphs as follows. Section 5.2.1 presents JOCL (Java bindings for OpenCL) [60], a Java library used by developers to offload computation on OpenCL devices. Section 5.2.2 shows an example of programming with JOCL. Section 5.2.3 describes how to code a two-dimensional computation for GPU execution and measure the performance. Finally, Sect. 5.2.4 highlights some takeaway remarks from using a wrapper interface.

5.2.1 Overview of the JOCL Library

This section describes how Java developers can use a wrapper interface to program GPUs. In particular, we use JOCL [60] as an example of a wrapper interface. JOCL is a library that implements an API to program hardware accelerators with OpenCL from Java. Besides JOCL, there is also the JCUDA library that exposes a wrapper interface for CUDA to Java developers.

JOCL provides a set of interfaces and classes that map to the OpenCL C data structures and standard runtime functions whenever possible. For example, many of the functions (e.g., `clCreateContext`, `clCreateCommandQueue`, etc.) in OpenCL create an object (e.g., context, command queue, etc.) which is later used by other OpenCL functions via a C/C++ pointer. However, pointers are not allowed/supported in Java. Thus, JOCL provides abstractions and utilities to perform that mapping between Java code and low-level OpenCL code.

> It is a good practice for developers to program their applications while following the specification of a programming model (e.g., OpenCL, CUDA, etc.). This can facilitate maintainers to keep track of new releases.

Figure 5.1 shows the workflow of the main software components that operate when a Java application uses the JOCL wrapper interface to offload a computation on GPUs. The JOCL library is composed of two parts: the JOCL API (depicted in red) used by the applications, and the native implementation of the JOCL library (depicted in green). The native implementation is usually distributed as a Java Native Interface (JNI) shared library (`dll`, `so`) that directly invokes OpenCL C routines using an OpenCL implementation (e.g., Intel OpenCL SDK). As shown in Fig. 5.1, developers are responsible for providing the OpenCL kernel functions

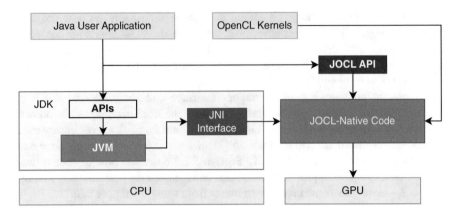

Fig. 5.1 Key software components of JOCL applications, and how they interact with JDK and the JVM

to be launched on the target accelerator and store the functions in a Java string type. The application is executed by a JVM distribution (e.g., OpenJDK). When the JVM invokes native calls to access the low-level routines of the JOCL library, it accesses native code and native memory directly. The following sections show that programming with JOCL, although it is from Java, requires developers to understand the GPU execution model and the OpenCL programming model. This is because explicit OpenCL C kernels are explicitly provided, and these kernels, although provided through a Java program, follow the OpenCL semantics.

5.2.2 Example of Programming with JOCL

The aim of this section is to demonstrate the use of the JOCL API from Java programs, and show how developers can create and launch new kernels. In particular, we will show an example of a Java program that offloads the computation of a square arithmetic operation on a GPU by using the JOCL API.

Before going through the description of the Java program, we will use in our project the `maven` tool to build the Java project and obtain all software dependencies. The JOCL dependency is added in the XML `pom` file of the Java project, as shown in Listing 5.1.

Listing 5.1 XML code for importing the JOCL Framework into a Java Maven project

```
1  <dependency>
2      <groupId>org.jocl</groupId>
3      <artifactId>jocl</artifactId>
4      <version>2.0.4</version>
5  </dependency>
```

> We are using the latest version available at the time of writing this book. However, further releases of JOCL may come in the future. Thus, we recommend following the main GitHub repository to checkout the latest version [60].

Now that we described the installation of the JOCL dependency, it is time to discuss how to program with JOCL. The OpenCL C kernel function that implements the computation of the square arithmetic operation of an input vector is shown in Listing 5.2. As mentioned earlier, developers must encapsulate the OpenCL C kernel into a Java string in order to invoke the kernel from Java with JOCL. Listing 5.3 shows an example of the Java string that contains the body kernel of Listing 5.2.

Listing 5.2 OpenCL C kernel for computing the square numbers of an input vector

```
1  __kernel__ void computeSquare(__global__ float* input,
2                                  __global__ float *output,
3                                  int size)
4  {
5      size_t idx = get_global_iodx(0);
6      if (idx < size) {
7          output[idx] = input[idx] * input[idx];
8      }
9  }
```

Listing 5.3 OpenCL C kernel stored in a String type in Java

```
1  String openclKernel = "__kernel__ void computeSquare(\n"+
2          "__global__ float* input,\n"+
3          "__global__ float *output,\n"+
4          "int size)\n"+
5          "{ \n" +
6          "size_t idx = get_global_iodx(0);\n" +
7          "if (idx < size) {\n" +
8          "    output[idx] = input[idx] * input[idx];\n" +
9          "}\n" +
10         "}";
```

Once the definition of the kernel is stored in a string type, it is necessary to implement some auxiliary tasks and some primary tasks that belong to the host code. To facilitate the reader, we follow the same definition of the tasks as discussed in Sect. 3.5.1.

Many of the OpenCL operations returns an error code, and other the error is controlled by an argument that is passed by reference. In JOCL, we can enable exceptions to indicate that, if there is an error, a Java exception will be raised instead. Listing 5.4 shows how exceptions are enabled for the JOCL runtime.

Listing 5.4 JOCL function call to raise exceptions for capturing the error codes

```
1   // Enable exceptions, and therefore, omit error checks in this
          ↪ sample
2   CL.setExceptionsEnabled(true);
```

The auxiliary tasks contain the discovery of the available platforms, the initialization of the input data as well as the validation of the result data from the GPU. The primary tasks are executed in six steps, as follows:

1. Initialize the OpenCL data structures (i.e., platform, device, context, command queue) along with the necessary data buffers.
2. Transfer input data from the host memory to device memory.
3. Create a kernel object from the string that stores the OpenCL C source and set up the arguments of the kernel.
4. Launch the execution of the created kernel object.
5. Transfer result data from device to host.
6. Release the allocated resources.

> Note that the tasks listed above are not exclusive to JOCL, and many other wrapper interfaces for GPU and FPGA programming expose similar tasks to programmers.

Step 1. Initialize the OpenCL Data Structures and Data Buffers

The first step presents how Java developers can use the JOCL library to initialize the fundamental data structures that are required to execute an OpenCL kernel. Thus, we start with the discovery of the number of platforms available in a computing system. Listing 5.5 shows the Java code that queries the OpenCL platforms in a system and retrieves a `cl_platform_id` object for a specific platform. More specifically, line 2 declares a Java array of one element size. The array is expected to store the final number of platforms that have been discovered.

The functions that implement the specification of a programming model (e.g., OpenCL, CUDA, etc.) return pointers to objects and in some cases a status code that reports whether an internal error has occurred. Unlike C and C++, Java does not support pointers and neither can directly access a memory address. A common practice is Java developers to use Java objects (e.g., a Java array) as parameters to the OpenCL native functions. Thus, developers can use the Java object to access the data that has been updated/modified during the execution of the low-level function.

In line 3 of Listing 5.5, the clGetPlatformIDs function that queries the number of platforms available in a computer system is invoked. The second argument of the function is a null reference to indicate to the OpenCL driver that the intention is to query the total number of OpenCL platforms. Once the number of platforms has been queried, developers can instance a Java array of type cl_platform_id and length equal to the total number of OpenCL platforms, as shown in line 7. To obtain an instance object of each OpenCL platforms, a new invocation to the clGetPlatformIDs function is performed. However, this time the second parameter is not null but the array of cl_platform_id. The definition of the second parameter as not null indicates the OpenCL runtime to populate the Java array with all the OpenCL platform objects.

Listing 5.5 Snippet of Java code using JOCL to access the OpenCL platform

```
1  // Obtain the number of platforms
2  int numPlatformsArray[] = new int[1];
3  CL.clGetPlatformIDs(0, null, numPlatformsArray);
4  int numPlatforms = numPlatformsArray[0];
5
6  // Obtain a platform ID
7  cl_platform_id platforms[] = new cl_platform_id[numPlatforms];
8  CL.clGetPlatformIDs(platforms.length, platforms, null);
9  cl_platform_id platform = platforms[platformIndex];
```

Once the array of platforms has been instantiated, we can obtain the list of devices associated with each platform. To obtain the instances of the devices, we follow a similar procedure to the aforementioned platform. Listing 5.6 shows the code snippet that performs the instantiation of the available OpenCL devices using the JOCL library. More specifically, line 3 invokes the clGetDeviceIDs function to query the total number of OpenCL devices that belong to a specific OpenCL platform. The number of OpenCL devices is stored in the first element of the Java array and then it is stored in a variable, as shown in line 4. Line 7 allocates a Java array to store all device references and line 8 invokes the clGetDeviceIDs function for a second time to obtain those references.

Listing 5.6 Snippet of Java code using JOCL to access the OpenCL list of devices for a specific OpenCL platform

```
1  // Obtain the number of devices for the platform
2  int numDevicesArray[] = new int[1];
3  CL.clGetDeviceIDs(platform, deviceType, 0, null, numDevicesArray
       ↪);
4  int numDevices = numDevicesArray[0];
5
6  // Obtain a device ID
7  cl_device_id devices[] = new cl_device_id[numDevices];
8  CL.clGetDeviceIDs(platform, deviceType, numDevices, devices, null
       ↪);
```

Now that the number of platforms along with the associated list of devices have been retrieved, developers can move to the creation of the OpenCL execution context and the OpenCL command queue objects. An OpenCL context can be created with one or many devices. Listing 5.7 shows an example of how to create an execution context with one device via the JOCL API. Thus, we use the device reference that was previously instantiated.

Listing 5.7 Snippet of Java code using JOCL to create an OpenCL execution context

```
1  // Create an Execution Context in JOCL
2  cl_context context = CL.clCreateContext(null,   // context
       ↪properties
3                                          1,       // number of
                                               ↪devices
4                                          new cl_device_id[]{device
                                               ↪}, // device list
5                                          null,   // callback
                                               ↪function
6                                          null,   // user data
7                                          null);  // return error
                                               ↪code
```

In turn, developers can use the references for the OpenCL device and the context to create an OpenCL command queue, as presented in Listing 5.8. Note that, although we can create an OpenCL context for multiple devices, each device has at least one command queue associated with it. This means that, if we create an OpenCL context object with two GPUs, we need to create one command queue per device.

Listing 5.8 Snippet of Java code using JOCL to create an OpenCL command queue

```
1  // Create an OpenCL Command Queue
2  cl_command_queue commandQueue = CL.clCreateCommandQueue(
3                          context,
4                          device,
5                          0,    // command queue properties
6                          null); // return error code
```

The next stage regards the initialization of the input and output data that is going to be used by the computation. Listing 5.9 shows a code snippet in Java that creates two arrays (`inputArray`, `outputArray`—lines 4–5), and initializes the content of the input array with random float numbers (line 13). The data in the arrays resides in the Java heap.

Additionally, lines 8–9 show how the JOCL API can expose native pointers for the allocated data in Java. This functionality is performed by invoking the `Pointer.to()` function. This function stores the native pointers that are associated to the Java object arrays in the JOCL `Pointer` object. Those pointers can be used later by the native implementation of the JOCL library (green box in Fig. 5.1), when data will be transferred from host to device, or backwards.

Listing 5.9 Host data allocation in Java and preparation for JOCL buffer allocation

```
1   final int SIZE = 100000;
2
3   // Allocate host data (data that will reside in the Java heap)
4   float[] inputArray = new float[SIZE];
5   float[] outputArray = new float[SIZE];
6
7   // Obtain native pointers to the data
8   Pointer srcA = Pointer.to(inputArray);
9   Pointer srcB = Pointer.to(outputArray);
10
11  Random r = new Random(31);
12  // Initialize the input array
13  IntStream.range(0, SIZE).forEach( i-> inputArray[i] = r.nextFloat());
```

Before transferring the data, developers must create the data buffers that are going to be used to move data between the main memory of the CPU and the device memory, as has been described in Sect. 3.4.1. This stage is necessary specifically if the accelerator devices do not share the memory with the host processor (i.e., CPU). Listing 5.10 shows the JOCL code used to allocate the OpenCL buffers. In the code snippet, we see that two buffers are allocated (`bufferA`, and `bufferB`) via the `clCreateBuffer` OpenCL function. In essence, this function call allocates a chunk of bytes on the accelerators global memory. This chunk of memory is outside the Java heap.

We pass the context as first parameter and then, we declare a set of flags that define the data flow in each buffer. In our example, we have one input array and one output array. Thus, we declare the input array as read-only and the output array as write-only. The classification of the data into *read* and *write* is important, because OpenCL vendors can implement optimizations to increase the efficiency of the data transfers. For example, if an array is declared as read-only, a GPU driver can copy the data to a specific memory region for constant memory on the GPU.

Additionally, lines 4 and 10 contain the CL_MEM_COPY_HOST_PTR flag which indicates that the data pointed by the fourth parameter should be copied to the allocated buffer. The fourth parameter (i.e., srcA, srcB) is of Pointer type. In a nutshell, the CL_MEM_COPY_HOST_PTR flag is used to avoid the explicit invocation of the clEnqueueWriteBuffer call for writing the data to a buffer. However, this can be valid if data are meant to be transferred once.

It is obvious that programming with wrapper interfaces, while offering high-level of control over the accelerators by exposing the OpenCL and CUDA functions to managed runtime environments, it also adds a burden to developers to allocate/deallocate the buffers and keep consistency between the data that reside in the main memory and the device memory. This can be further exacerbated if someone considers also the impact of GC when trying to maintain data consistency.

Listing 5.10 Device buffer allocation and data transfers in JOCL

```
1   // Create OpenCL Buffers
2   // 1) OpenCL buffer for the input array
3   cl_mem bufferA = CL.clCreateBuffer(context,
4                                       CL.CL_MEM_READ_ONLY | CL.
                                          ↪CL_MEM_COPY_HOST_PTR,
5                                       Sizeof.cl_float * SIZE,
6                                       srcA,
7                                       null);
8   // 2) OpenCL buffer for the output array, in which we expect the
        ↪result
9   cl_mem bufferB = CL.clCreateBuffer(context,
10                                      CL.CL_MEM_WRITE_ONLY | CL.
                                          ↪CL_MEM_COPY_HOST_PTR,
11                                      Sizeof.cl_float * SIZE,
12                                      srcB,
13                                      null);
```

Step 2. Transfer Input Data from Host to Device

The second step shows how to express the transferring of input data from the main memory of the CPU to the device memory. The JOCL API exposes the OpenCL commands for transferring input data to Java developers. Note that those commands have been already discussed in Sect. 3.4.2.

Listing 5.11 shows a code snippet, in Java, for transferring the data of the input array (inputArray) from the host memory to the device memory. To facilitate the reader, the code snippet includes the allocation of the OpenCL buffer (`deviceBuffer`) that is associated for this data transfer in lines 2–6. In turn, lines 8–17 express the invocation of the OpenCL write buffer command (`clEnqueueWriteBuffer`) from Java. As shown in those lines, developers can configure all the arguments of the native OpenCL function that performs this operation. In addition, developers are responsible for expressing all the arguments of the native OpenCL function that performs this operation. Thus, they should be aware of how to use the OpenCL programming model because they can control many configurations, including:

- Data offset in bytes in the buffer object to write the data to. Thus, it is possible to copy a subset of the input array to the buffer object in the device memory.
- Blocking or non-blocking call. This is significant to enable or disable asynchronous data movements.
- Declaration of list of events to wait for. This mechanism is employed to show that this command has a dependency to other commands, by using the events of those commands in the wait list.

Listing 5.11 Data transfer from the host to the device in JOCL

```
1   // Create a device buffer without the host pointer back-up array.
2   cl_mem deviceBuffer = CL.clCreateBuffer(context,
3                   CL.CL_MEM_READ_ONLY,
4                   Sizeof.cl_float * SIZE,
5                   null,
6                   null);
7   // Data transfer from Host -> Device
8   int status = CL.clEnqueueWriteBuffer(
9           commandQueue, // command queue
10          deviceBuffer, // device buffer
11          CL.CL_TRUE,   // blocking operation
12          0,            // offset
13          Sizeof.cl_float * SIZE, // size to be transferred
14          Pointer.to(inputArray), // pointer to data
15          0,                      // events to wait
16          null,                   // list of events to wait
17          null);                  // new event for the current call
```

Non-blocking execution of OpenCL commands is used to enable asynchronous execution, which can improve the utilization of computing resources and the overlap of data transfers with computation. Thus, it can increase the performance of OpenCL applications. The OpenCL specification defines which commands support blocking and non-blocking operations. It is in the responsibility of the developer to ensure that the functionality of the application is correct (i.e., no memory issues or segmentation faults), if non-blocking operations are enabled.

In line 11, we defined the write operation to be blocking since the input data is allocated in the heap, hence it can be moved by the GC (Sect. 4.3). Therefore, the JOCL documentation reports that non-blocking operations must be avoided when using on-heap data (e.g., Java arrays) [68]. If developers want to perform non-blocking operations, they should allocate the data off-heap. In a nutshell, Java, and many managed languages, offer APIs (e.g., the Panama Foreign Function and Memory (FFM) API [83], the ByteBuffer API, etc.) to access data that is not reachable by the GC. Nonetheless, a drawback of this approach is that developers are responsible for the memory management of the data, i.e., allocation and deallocation.

Step 3. Create a Kernel Object and Set the Arguments

The next step is to create an OpenCL program that contains the OpenCL kernels and create a kernel object for each kernel to be launched. That functionality has been described in Sect. 3.4.3 (Fig. 3.3). Listing 5.12 shows a code snippet that performs the creation and building of the OpenCL program (lines 2–7) and the creation of the kernel object (lines 19–22). To build the OpenCL program we used the clCreateProgramWithSource function, since the OpenCL kernel is in the form of a source file stored in a string type (Listing 5.3). Once the program object is created, it is compiled as shown in line 10. Note that, optionally, developers can specify many devices for which the kernel should be compiled (lines 12–13). The reason is that an OpenCL context can be associated with one or many OpenCL devices. In our example, we do not specify any specific device in line 13 which results in compiling the kernel for all devices.

If the OpenCL kernel has been compiled with no errors, then an OpenCL kernel object can be created via the clCreateKernel function for each kernel. In our example we compile only one kernel (Listing 5.2).

> Note that users may encounter a correct Java program that calls an invalid OpenCL program and they will only receive the error message at runtime. The reason is that the application is divided in two parts: the host code (Java code running on the CPU), and the device code (the kernel running on an accelerator). Thus, the OpenCL kernel is compiled at runtime.

Listing 5.12 OpenCL program builder in JOCL

```
1   // Create the program from the source code
2   cl_program program = CL.clCreateProgramWithSource(
3       context,        // OpenCL context
4       1,              // Number of OpenCL C files
5       new String[]{ openclSquareProgram },   // Array of OpenCL C
            ↪programs
6       null,           // lenghts
7       null);          // error code
8
9   // Build the program: it invokes the OpenCL JIT compiler
10  status = CL.clBuildProgram(
11      program,        // OpenCL program object
12      0,              // number of devices (0 means compile for all
            ↪devices)
13      null,           // device list
14      null,           // compiler options
15      null,           // call back function
16      null);          // user data to the call back function
17
18  // Create the kernel object
19  cl_kernel kernel = CL.clCreateKernel(
20      program,        // OpenCL program
21      "square",       // Kernel function name
22      null);          // error code
```

The kernel object that is generated in Listing 5.12 is going to be used to set the arguments of the kernel. As shown in Listing 5.3, the OpenCL kernel of our example has three arguments. The first argument is the input array, the second argument is the output array and the last argument is the size of the arrays. Listing 5.13 shows the Java code that sets the arguments for the OpenCL kernel. The function clSetKernelArg is invoked three times in lines 3–5; one per argument.

Extra care is required when dealing with the types of the arguments passed in the clSetKernelArg as last parameter. In lines 3–4, we pass an OpenCL buffer as an argument, and thus, a Pointer type should be used and the size of the argument is cl_mem. Whereas, in line 5 we pass an int array that stores the constant value SIZE in the first element. In this case, a Pointer type is also used but the size of the argument is cl_uint.

Listing 5.13 Java code snippet that shows how to setup the total numnber of threads before launching the OpenCL kernel

```
1   // Set the arguments for the kernels
2   int argId = 0;
3   CL.clSetKernelArg(kernel, argId++, Sizeof.cl_mem, Pointer.to(
        ↪bufferA));
4   CL.clSetKernelArg(kernel, argId++, Sizeof.cl_mem, Pointer.to(
        ↪bufferB));
5   CL.clSetKernelArg(kernel, argId++, Sizeof.cl_uint, Pointer.to(new
        ↪ int[]{SIZE}));
```

The sizes of the arrays (last argument of the kernel) are not required by the kernel, but it is a common practice in OpenCL to check that illegal memory is not accessed. Since we map the array size to the total number of threads, adding this extra check in the kernel guarantees that the GPU kernel does not access illegal positions of the array at runtime.

Step 4. Launch the Execution of the Kernel Object

In this step we show how an OpenCL kernel is launched for execution. The first part is the configuration of the grid dimensions and the work group size. The kernel of our example is a one-dimensional kernel and it does not use any data stored in local memory. Thus, we only need to define the total number of threads as the global work group size. Optionally, we can also define the local work group size. The definitions of the global and local work group sizes are already given in Sect. 3.4.3. This part is very important for the following reasons:

1. The selection of the right size of work groups (global/local) can increase performance.
2. If the application uses data stored in local memory, it is a common practice to launch as local work group size the size of the data stored in local memory. However, the capacity of the local memory is limited. Thus, developers need to understand the limitations of the accelerators, and select the most appropriate work group size that is tailored to each case.

Listing 5.14 Java code snippet that shows how to setup the total number of threads before launching the OpenCL kernel

```
1  // Set the work-item dimensions
2  long global_work_size[] = new long[]{SIZE};
```

The second part invokes the `clEnqueueNDRangeKernel` OpenCL command that offloads the kernel for execution, as shown in Listing 5.15. The arguments of that command are the command queue, the kernel object and the number of threads (global and local) to be launched. The last arguments of the `clEnqueueNDRangeKernel` command are related to the list of the events to await.

Listing 5.15 Java code snippet that shows how to launch an OpenCL kernel using the JOCL wrapper framework

```
1  // Execute the OpenCL kernel
2  CL.clEnqueueNDRangeKernel(
3      commandQueue,      // command queue
4      kernel,            // kernel object
5      1,                 // dimentions {1D, 2D, 3D}
```

```
6     null,                // global offset
7     global_work_size,    // global work size = total number of
          ↪threads per dimension
8     null,                // local work size (block size )
9     0,                   // number of events to wait
10    null,                // list of events to wait for
11    null);               // new kernel event
```

The `clEnqueueNDRangeKernel` function is essential for launching parallel computations on OpenCL devices. It allows us to specify several configurations of how the kernel is going to be executed, including the range of *work-items*, *work-groups*, event dependencies, etc. Additionally, note that this function is not a blocking call, thus developers need to wait for the kernel to be completed before performing any subsequent operations. To achieve this, developers can wait for the kernel event to be completed, or flush the OpenCL command queue.

Step 5. Transfer Result Data from Device to Host

This step concerns the transferring of the result data from the device memory back to the main memory of the CPU. Listing 5.16 shows a code snippet in Java that uses the `clEnqueueReadBuffer` function for transferring the data of the output array (`outputArray`). The arguments of that function call are the same with the corresponding arguments of the `clEnqueueWriteBuffer` function (used in Step 2). To guarantee that the result data (`outputArray`) can be accessed after the invocation of this the `clEnqueueReadBuffer` function, we configure the operation as a blocking call (line 5).

Listing 5.16 Java code snippet to read the results from the GPU execution

```
1   // Read the output data
2   CL.clEnqueueReadBuffer(
3       commandQueue,        // command queue
4       bufferB,             // result buffer
5       CL.CL_TRUE,          // blocking call
6       0,                   // offset
7       SIZE * Sizeof.cl_float,   // data size
8       srcB,                // buffer on the host side
9       0,                   // num events to wait for
10      null,                // list of events
11      null);               // read event
```

Step 6. Release of Allocated Resources

As a final step, developers must deallocate the allocated memory objects that have been created for the execution of the OpenCL kernel. Listing 5.17 presents the calls that release all the objects that were created in our example.

Listing 5.17 Clean-up and memory de-allocation in JOCL

```
1  // Release kernel, program, and memory objects
2  CL.clReleaseMemObject(bufferA);
3  CL.clReleaseMemObject(bufferB);
4  CL.clReleaseKernel(kernel);
5  CL.clReleaseProgram(program);
6  CL.clReleaseCommandQueue(commandQueue);
7  CL.clReleaseContext(context);
```

Summary

This example has shown the different parts of a Java program using the JOCL parallel programming framework. Those parts are similar to the parts of a C/C++ program using OpenCL, as discussed in Chap. 3. The benefit of this approach is that Java developers have full control over the data handler and how the kernels are launched and computed. In the next section, we will present another example to perform a 2D computation in Java and JOCL, and start measuring the performance of the OpenCL kernels.

5.2.3 Launching Two-Dimensional Kernels in JOCL and Performance Evaluation

This section presents a second example of computation that utilizes two dimensions. In particular, it describes the implementation of a matrix multiplication application that offloads the computation on a GPU device via the JOCL API, and evaluates the performance of the hardware accelerated application against the functionally equivalent sequential implementation in Java.

Java Sequential Implementation of Matrix Multiplication

Listing 5.18 presents a sequential Java implementation of the canonical matrix multiplication algorithm. This implementation contains three loops that iterate over the rows and columns of both input matrices to perform a `matrix-vector` computation in the innermost loop (lines 4–6). This example computes the matrix multiplication of two square matrices (i.e., the size of the rows is equal to size of columns).

Additionally, the example uses the data of the input matrices flattened in one dimension. We make this decision for two reasons: (1) We want to use this code to compare directly with the OpenCL kernel; (2) contrary to C and C++, Java arrays are objects that point to objects. If we think about the rows and columns of a matrix in Java, each row element references another array. Since OpenCL does not support objects, we provide a flattened memory region to read/write data.

If developers want to use explicit two-dimensional arrays from Java, they will need to either perform data marshalling and unmarshalling, or provide access to two-dimensional array objects within the OpenCL kernels. The second option may introduce a performance overhead due to misaligned and non-coalesced memory accesses within the memory of an accelerator (e.g., a GPU).

Listing 5.18 Sequential Java implementation of the classic algorithm for Matrix Multiplication

```
1  for (int ic = 0; ic < SIZE; ic++) {
2      for (int j = 0; j < SIZE; j++) {
3          float acc = 0.0f;
4          for (int k = 0; k < SIZE; k++) {
5              acc += matrixA[ic * SIZE + k] * matrixB[k * SIZE + j];
6          }
7          resultC[ic * SIZE + j] = acc;
8      }
9  }
```

OpenCL Kernel of Matrix Multiplication

Based on the Java code snippet of the matrix multiplication implementation shown in Listing 5.18, this paragraph describes a parallel implementation in OpenCL. The matrix multiplication example can be represented as a two-dimensional kernel, and take advantage of the thread-id indexing of two dimensions to access data and compute in parallel. Listing 5.19 shows the OpenCL C kernel of matrix multiplication that is functionally equivalent to the Java implementation described in Listing 5.18. The kernel has four arguments: three arrays that correspond to the two input arrays and one output array that stores the result, and one constant value that stores the size of the matrices.

As we explained in Chaps. 2 and 3, parallel programming models such as OpenCL, CUDA and oneAPI express the computation in the form of dimensions (1D, 2D and 3D). Two-dimensional and three-dimensional kernels are abstractions to ease programmability and data access patterns in parallel kernel implementations. The GPU drivers will take these abstractions and map them to a one-dimensional dimension.

If we inspect the sequential implementation of the matrix multiplication shown in Listing 5.18, each iteration of the two outermost loops can be computed independently. Then, the work to be done per thread is the reduction loop from lines 4–6 of Listing 5.18. In lines 8 and 9 of Listing 5.19, we obtain the thread-ids for each dimension, and we use these ids to access the matrices, as we see in line 14. In between, we compute the matrix-vector operation.

Listing 5.19 OpenCL C kernel for the classic algorithms of Matrix Multiplication

```
1   private static String openclMatrixMultiplicationProgram =
2       "__kernel void "+
3       "   mxm(__global const float *a, "+
4       "       __global const float *b, " +
5       "       __global float *c, " +
6       "       const int size) " +
7       "{ "+
8       "    int idx = get_global_id(0); "+
9       "    int idy = get_global_id(1); "+
10      "    float sum = 0.0f; "+
11      "    for (int k = 0; k < size; k++) { "+
12      "        sum += a[idx * size + k] * b[k * size + idy]; "+
13      "    } "+
14      "    c[idx * size + idy] = sum; "+
15      "} ";
```

Launching Two-Dimensional Kernels

Five out of the six steps that we discussed in Sect. 5.2.2 are similar with the steps being implemented in this example too. The only significant difference regards the fourth step that launches the execution of the kernel. Thus, this paragraph will describe that step. The source code of the implementation described in this section is available in GitHub [59].

Listing 5.20 shows the code snippet for launching the two-dimensional OpenCL kernel to compute matrix multiplication. The first line creates an array that stores the size of the global work group per dimension; thus, the array contains two elements. The OpenCL command to launch the kernel (line 2) is the same as in the previous example, but it has different configuration this time. In particular, the third argument (line 5) defines two as the number of dimensions used by the kernel, and the array that stores the global work size (line 7) has two elements.

Listing 5.20 Launching a two-dimensional kernel for the Matrix Multiplication in JOCL

```
1   long[] global_work_size = new long[]{SIZE, SIZE};
2   CL.clEnqueueNDRangeKernel(
3       commandQueue,
4       kernel,
5       2,          // Number of dimensions
6       null,
7       global_work_size,
8       null,
9       0,
10      null,
11      kernelEvent);
```

Measuring the Kernel Execution Time

This paragraph discusses how developers can measure the execution time of a kernel, once the kernel is launched. Note that the launch and the actual execution of a kernel may not happen instantly (Sect. 3.4.3). In addition, the time spent in the MRE (i.e., the JVM) to execute the native OpenCL function and return back can be significant.

Listing 5.21 shows how to launch the OpenCL kernel (via clEnqueueNDRange Kernel), and use an OpenCL event (kernelEvent) that we can use at a later stage during the execution. The reason is because this function is not a blocking function by definition, and we want to ensure when the kernel has finished the execution to measure the elapsed kernel time. Therefore, we have added in line 5 a blocking call to the CL.clWaitForEvents JOCL function, which waits till the input event is completed.

Listing 5.21 Possible approach to measure the OpenCL kernel execution time

```
1   long start = System.nanoTime();
2   cl_event kernelEvent;
3   CL.clEnqueueNDRangeKernel(commandQueue,  kernel, 2, null,
4               global_work_size, null, 0, null, kernelEvent);
5   CL.waitForEvents(1, new cl_kernel[]{kernelEvent});
6   long end = System.nanoTime();
```

To measure the elapsed time for the kernel execution in Java, we added two system calls in lines 1 and 6 that return the time stamp in nanoseconds. Nonetheless, there is a more precise way to measure the execution time of a kernel in OpenCL by also using the kernel event. To utilize this way, the command queue must have been created with the configuration of the profiling information enabled as shown in Listing 5.22.

Listing 5.22 JOCL code to create an OpenCL command queue with profiling information enabled

```
1  cl_command_queue commandQueue = CL.clCreateCommandQueue(
2      context,
3      device,
4      CL.CL_QUEUE_PROFILING_ENABLE,   // enable profiling
5      null);
```

Consequently, developers can obtain the kernel execution time by invoking the JOCL function `CL.clGetEventProfilingInfo` as shown in Listing 5.23. This function returns the device time counter in nanoseconds, and it can be used to query various metrics, including when a command is submitted to a queue, started, finished, etc. Therefore, it can be used not only for measuring the kernel execution time, but also the time of transferring data from host to device, and backwards. Lines 6–7 retrieve the time counter when the kernel execution command started, whereas lines 10–11 return the time counter when the command finished. Line 12 subtracts the two timers to calculate the actual duration of the kernel execution.

Listing 5.23 JOCL code to obtain the elapsed time for the GPU kernel execution

```
1  // Wait for the kernel to finish before collecting profiling info
2  CL.clWaitForEvents(1, new cl_event[]{kernelEvent});
3
4  // 1. Obtain the start timestamp of the execution
5  long[] start = new long[1];
6  CL.clGetEventProfilingInfo(kernelEvent, CL.
      ↪CL_PROFILING_COMMAND_START,
7                                  Sizeof.cl_long, Pointer.to(start),
                                      ↪null);
8  long[] end = new long[1];
9  // 2. Obtain the end timestamp of the execution
10 CL.clGetEventProfilingInfo(kernelEvent, CL.
      ↪CL_PROFILING_COMMAND_END,
11                                 Sizeof.cl_long, Pointer.to(end),
                                      ↪null);
12 parallelTotalTimers[i] = end[0] - start[0];
13
14 // The elapsed time is in nanoseconds
15 System.out.print("Parallel Kernel Time (ns) = " +
      ↪parallelTotalTimers[i]);
```

Performance Evaluation

In this paragraph, we aim to compare, in terms of performance, the execution of the Java sequential implementation of matrix multiplication against the JOCL implementation that will offload the computation on a GPU. Our example runs the parallel GPU kernel and the Java sequential implementation for several iterations and reports their time. The application trace of the example is presented in

Listing 5.24, and the accelerator card is an NVIDIA RTX 2060 GPU. The GPU is able to execute the multiplication of two matrices of 1024×1024 elements up to $34\times$ faster than the Java sequential implementation. The trace shows the execution of the implemented Java application on a Linux machine (Fedora 34) with the NVIDIA driver 510.54 installed. This information is important because performance can be different on different OS distributions, and driver versions.

Listing 5.24 Execution of the Matrix Multiplication example with JOCL running on an NVIDIA RTX 2060 on Fedora 34

```
 1  -----------------------------------
 2  Using OpenCL platform: NVIDIA CUDA
 3  Device Name: NVIDIA GeForce RTX 2060
 4  -----------------------------------
 5  Parallel Kernel Time (ns) = 68796416 Java Sequential Time (ns) =
      ↪1465503236
 6  Parallel Kernel Time (ns) = 75286944 Java Sequential Time (ns) =
      ↪1566521800
 7  Parallel Kernel Time (ns) = 75280576 Java Sequential Time (ns) =
      ↪1530643441
 8  Parallel Kernel Time (ns) = 77477888 Java Sequential Time (ns) =
      ↪1534603851
 9  Parallel Kernel Time (ns) = 76442752 Java Sequential Time (ns) =
      ↪1528932201
10  Parallel Kernel Time (ns) = 69019296 Java Sequential Time (ns) =
      ↪1528857543
11  Parallel Kernel Time (ns) = 76437472 Java Sequential Time (ns) =
      ↪1530328061
12  Parallel Kernel Time (ns) = 79237120 Java Sequential Time (ns) =
      ↪1528608237
13  Parallel Kernel Time (ns) = 76439552 Java Sequential Time (ns) =
      ↪1530894256
14  Parallel Kernel Time (ns) = 76436704 Java Sequential Time (ns) =
      ↪1526408616
15  Parallel Kernel Time (ns) = 76440544 Java Sequential Time (ns) =
      ↪1527658668
16  Parallel Kernel Time (ns) = 76439648 Java Sequential Time (ns) =
      ↪1527993716
17  Parallel Kernel Time (ns) = 80892128 Java Sequential Time (ns) =
      ↪1581392746
18  Parallel Kernel Time (ns) = 77227872 Java Sequential Time (ns) =
      ↪1691526128
19  Parallel Kernel Time (ns) = 42983424 Java Sequential Time (ns) =
      ↪1662251939
20  OpenCL program finished
21  JOCL TIMERS
22  Min     : 42983424
23  Max     : 80892128
24  Average : 7.365588906666666E7
25  Variance: 7.657211346259514E13
26  STD     : 8750549.323476506
27
28
```

```
29  JAVA TIMERS
30  Min     : 1465503236
31  Max     : 1691526128
32  Average : 1.5508082959333334E9
33  Variance: 3.018045381299891E15
34  STD     : 5.4936739813169576E7
```

In this section it has been showcased that developers who exploit hardware acceleration do not only need to have a good understanding of hardware architecture, but also own performance engineering skills. Since this book focuses on programmability and the challenges posed when programming hardware accelerators from MREs, readers should consider to study performance caveats and performance engineering of heterogeneous computing architectures as a complementary material [98–100].

5.2.4 Remarks of GPU Programming via the JOCL Wrapper Interface

One important consideration when programming with wrapper interfaces is that developers are responsible for the memory management and the compilation of the compute function, despite writing their application in a managed programming language. The reason is that the wrapper interfaces expose to managed languages the functionality of non-managed and native languages such as C and C++. Consequently, developers should be aware of parallel programming as well as the execution model of the heterogeneous programming models in order to use the accelerators efficiently. Beneath, we present some takeaway notes to keep in mind:

- **Not single-source development:** Even though applications are programmed in a managed language, developers are required to explicitly define the kernel functions as string types. This style of programming is not necessarily bad, however, it impacts the productivity of developers who are required to implement and maintain two different programs (i.e., a host program implemented in a managed language, and the kernel function implemented in OpenCL C) in order to use hardware accelerators.
- **Non-blocking calls allowed:** As shown in previous paragraphs, developers who use a wrapper interface (e.g., JOCL) to exploit hardware acceleration from an MRE, such as the JVM, must be careful with the management of data that reside in the heap. The reason is that heterogeneous programming models require data to be transferred from the heap to the device memory, thereby making developers responsible for keeping the data consistent between both sides. This can add an

extra burden to developers, considering that the data in the heap are moved during a GC cycle. Thus, the JOCL framework declares that non-blocking operations must be avoided when using on-heap data.

- **Supported data types:** In general, there is an inconsistency between the objects defined in a managed language and the supported types of a heterogeneous programming model. In JOCL, and other wrapper interfacing libraries, developers can use only a subset of Java objects. Thus, developers must be aware of the supported types and how to send/receive data to/from the accelerator.

5.3   Programming with Software Libraries that Use Prebuilt Kernel Functions

A second approach to exploit hardware acceleration from managed runtime environments is by employing software libraries that use internally prebuilt kernel functions. These libraries expose APIs to developers that are usually composed of various data structures and operations. The data structures are used by developers to shape the data of a program in a specific form. For instance, a *tensor* is a data structure widely used in deep learning to represent data as an array of floating point numbers. The operations are used by developers to express the type of data processing in a hardware agnostic manner. If an operation can exploit hardware acceleration to run faster, the library implicitly employs prebuilt kernel implementations provided by hardware vendor libraries.

The kernel implementations provided by hardware vendors (e.g., NVIDIA, AMD, Intel, etc.) are optimized to execute efficiently on accelerators. Prime examples of those vendor libraries are NVIDIA cuDNN [36] and CUBLAS [33] as well as Intel oneDNN [34] and oneMKL [35] which contain kernel implementations of various operations, such as convolution, matrix multiplication, neuron activations (forward and backward), etc. The vast majority of those kernels is widely used to increase the performance in the domain of AI and Deep Learning. An additional example of FPGA prebuilt kernels is the AMD Vitis Accelerated Libraries [37].

Figure 5.2 illustrates the workflow of the main software components that operate when a program running atop an MRE uses a software library to leverage prebuilt kernel implementations. In this particular figure, we show a Java program running on top of the JVM. However, any other managed languages running on other MREs (e.g., .NET, Python Runtime Environment) can employ similar workflows.

As shown in Fig. 5.2, the software library exposes an API (red box) to developers at the application layer. Subsequently, the API functions map to inner operations that are not exposed to developers. The inner operations can be related to the execution model of the heterogeneous programming models or their internal blocks (Sect. 3.4), such as the allocation of data structures and data buffers, the dispatching of kernels, data transfers, etc. Those operations are implemented as native functions in the native layer of an MRE (green box in Fig. 5.2). For instance, the native functions

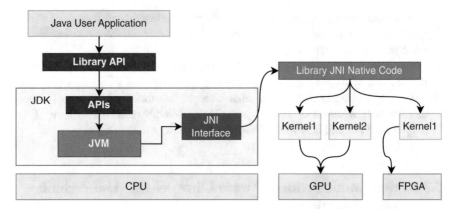

Fig. 5.2 Key software components of Software Libraries that use prebuilt kernels, and how they interact with Java and the JVM

in the JVM would be implemented in C/C++ and would be accessed by the MRE via the JNI (Sect. 4.2.4). The native functions are specific to the heterogeneous programming model supported by the vendor library. For example, if a software library uses the NVIDIA cuDNN kernels, the native functions are tailored to the CUDA specification. Thus, the software libraries are usually shipped along with the prebuilt kernels and the runtime implementation (including the driver) of the programming model that is supported.

An advantage of this approach is that developers are not required to explicitly program an accelerator card, thereby resulting in high code productivity. However, in this approach hardware acceleration comes at the cost of vendor lock-in since only particular devices from particular vendors are supported by the hardware vendor libraries.

Furthermore, although this approach has enabled developers to exploit hardware acceleration without requiring the explicit programming of the kernels, the challenge posed by the MRE regarding memory management is still present. Remember that data stored in the heap can be moved by the GC at runtime (Sect. 4.3). To circumvent this issue, some software libraries allocate the data structures that are being exposed to developers via their API off-heap. One prime example of this approach is PyTorch, a Python programming framework for Machine Learning and Deep Learning applications that exploit GPU hardware. PyTorch makes use of the Numpy library, which offers arrays and multi-dimensional matrices that are stored in off-heap memory. The PyTorch runtime system and data handler access those arrays to be sent to the accelerators, such as GPUs. Additionally, the data structures used internally by the libraries for inner operations (e.g., the buffer allocation, data transfers, and data synchronization) are also allocated off-heap. Thus, the data transferred between the host and an accelerator are not being moved by the GC.

The following sections describe two Python libraries that implicitly exploit hardware acceleration via employing hardware vendor libraries of prebuilt kernels. Section 5.3.1 presents ArrayFire [94], a Python interface for accelerating vector and matrix operations. Section 5.3.2 discusses PyTorch [45, 95], one of the most popular libraries used in machine learning and deep learning. Finally, Sect. 5.3.3 summarizes some takeaway remarks from this category.

5.3.1 Programming with ArrayFire

ArrayFire [94] is an open source software library for parallel computing that exploits hardware acceleration. ArrayFire exposes to developers an API of functions and data structures (e.g., tensor, multi-dimensional arrays, etc.) used to express computations that achieve high performance. The ArrayFire API is used in several application domains, including linear algebra, machine learning, computer vision, and signal processing. The ArrayFire library supports many heterogeneous programming models (e.g., CUDA, OpenCL, Metal, oneAPI) to offload computations on multi-core CPUs and GPUs.

The library abstracts away any information related to heterogeneous programming models, thereby making it easier and more productive for programmers to develop their programs. Nonetheless, ArrayFire allows developers to query device information and select a target device. But it handles the internal blocks (e.g., context, command queue, etc.) required by the execution model of the programming model in an automatic manner. The following paragraph describes an example developed with the ArrayFire library to compute a matrix multiplication.

Example of Programming with ArrayFire

The ArrayFire library can be installed in a computing system by using the `pip` Python Package manager. Listing 5.25 lists the command for installing the latest ArrayFire version at the time of writing this book. To install a different version, reader will have to change the version id and/or the corresponding CUDA version. The installed package enables us to use all ArrayFire functions with CUDA support for NVIDIA GPUs.

Listing 5.25 Installation of ArrayFire module for Python

```
1  $ pip install arrayfire==3.8.0+cu112 \
2     -f https://repo.arrayfire.com/python/wheels/3.8.0/
```

Listing 5.26 presents a Python program that multiplies two square matrices that contain 1024 elements. The first step that is executed is to import the ArrayFire library (line 1). Line 2 imports the `time` module that will be use to measure the elapsed time of our program (lines 11 and 14). Then, line 4 sets the CUDA backend to be used by the ArrayFire library to launch computation on NVIDIA GPUs. That step invokes all the inner operations required by the ArrayFire runtime system for accessing CUDA devices.

Subsequently, line 8 creates a matrix (A) of size 1024 × 1024. Note that this function creates a type provided by the ArrayFire API, and stored outside of the Python's heap area. Lines 10–15 iterates over a loop that computes the matrix multiplication and measures the elapsed time.

Listing 5.26 Matrix Multiplication Execution implemented in Python using the ArrayFire library

```
1   import arrayfire as af
2   import time
3
4   af.set_backend('cuda')
5   print(af.info_str())
6
7   ## Declare a matrix of 1024x1024
8   A = af.randu(1024, 1024)
9
10  for i in range(1,10):
11      start = time.time()
12      A2 = af.matmul(A, A)
13      af.sync()
14      end = time.time()
15      print(str(end - start) + " (s)")
```

At this stage, we can draw the following conclusions:

- Developers must select the backend to be used by the library, as shown in line 4.
- Developers do not need to explicitly write the code for allocating the data in the CUDA data buffers and launching the CUDA kernels. This functionality is internally handled by the ArrayFire library.
- Developers must be familiar with the layout of the new data types so that to port any existing code bases to ArrayFire.

Listing 5.27 presents the execution trace when running the program on an NVIDIA RTX 2060 GPU. The first time that the program runs the reported execution time is 1329 microseconds. On the other hand, the time reported for the following executions is 680 microseconds. This behavior is attributed to the fact that ArrayFire prepares the environment for the GPU and transfers the initial data in the first execution. Furthermore, the CUDA kernels are compiled by the GPU driver at runtime. After the first execution, the environment has been prepared, the code has been compiled and the data have been transferred to the device.

Listing 5.27 Execution trace of the Python program in Listing 5.26

```
1   ArrayFire v3.8.0 (CUDA 64bit)
2   [0] : NVIDIA_GeForce_RTX_2060_with_Max-Q_Design (Compute 7.5)
3
4   0.0013298988342285156 (s)
5   0.0007691383361816406 (s)
6   0.0006806850433349609 (s)
7   0.0006794929504394531 (s)
8   0.0006818771362304688 (s)
9   0.0006754398345947266 (s)
10  0.0006802082061767578 (s)
11  0.0006766319274902344 (s)
12  0.0006771087646484375 (s)
```

5.3.2 Programming with PyTorch

PyTorch is an open source library in Python developed by Meta Research for deep learning. PyTorch belongs to this category of libraries because it provides a high level API to developers, while implicitly invoking prebuilt kernels to run efficiently. Developers can use the PyTorch API to express tensor operators, create neural networks (NN), utilize an automatic differentiation library (i.e., `Autograph`). At the same time, PyTorch contains a runtime implementation that invokes prebuilt kernel functions that map to the API operations. This model is similar to the one exposed in Fig. 5.2.

> Python is a domain specific library designed for the development of Machine and Deep Learning applications. Thus, this book does not explain the data structures and functions exposed by the PyTorch API. To study PyTorch and comprehend its data structures and functions, we point readers to the following book [95].

Remember, this book has at its scope to describe the approaches used by developers to exploit hardware acceleration from a programming language that runs on top of an MRE. To that end, we provide a list of steps required to write an example program in Python with PyTorch:

1. Import the necessary dependencies and packages in the Python program.
2. Obtain the training data set.
3. Build a model. For example, create a neural network (NN) model.

4. Set up a loss and an optimization function.
5. Train the model by using the training data set.
6. Test the model with data that is not contained in the training data set.

The input and output of the trained model is represented by a *tensor* type. The computation that is usually offloaded on a GPU is provided by a prebuilt kernel implementation from a hardware vendor library (e.g., NVIDIA cuDNN [36]). GPUs are suitable hardware accelerators used during the training of a model to run tensor operations. Thus, the data pre-processing and post-processing parts of a program usually run on the CPU, while the tensor operation is executed on the GPU.

Example of Programming with PyTorch

Listing 5.28 shows the code snippet of a Python program that uses PyTorch to multiply a vector by a scalar value. The first line imports the PyTorch library in the program. In turn, line 4 uses the `tensor` function of the PyTorch library to create a vector and transfer the data to a CUDA buffer allocated in the GPU memory. Line 7 performs the multiplication which is automatically executed on the GPU. Finally, line 10 invokes the `cpu()` function of the tensor object to transfer the result of the multiplication from the GPU memory back to the CPU memory.

Listing 5.28 Python program using PyTorch to multiply a vector by a scalar value. The computation is performed on an NVIDIA GPU using CUDA

```
 1  import torch
 2
 3  # Create a tensor in PyTorch and move it to the GPU
 4  x = torch.tensor([1.0, 2.0, 3.0]).cuda()
 5
 6  # Perform operations on the GPU using tensors
 7  y = x * 2
 8
 9  # Transfer the tensor from the GPU to the CPU
10  y_cpu = y.cpu()
```

PyTorch avoids the impact of GC by allocating the data structures off-heap. For instance, one way to create a tensor in PyTorch is from the well-known data structure of the Numpy array (via `torch.from_numpy()`). The Numpy arrays are stored off-heap [95]. Thus, the GC used in Python cannot access those objects.

Furthermore, we build a second program that creates a neural network with PyTorch and performs the training of the model on a GPU. Listing 5.29 shows the code snippet of a pseudocode that describes the process of building a model in PyTorch. In particular, lines 1–2 import the necessary modules. Lines 4–7 build the model, whereas line 10 sends the model to be computed on the GPU via the cuda function.

Listing 5.29 Pseudocode of a NN model implemented in PyTorch. The training of the model is computed on a GPU. The example illustrated in this code snippet is not complete but illustrates the main steps

```
1   import torch
2   import torch.nn as nn
3
4   class MyModel(nn.Module):
5       def __init__(self):
6           super(MyModel, self).__init__()
7           self.fc = nn.Linear(10, 5)
8
9   # Create model and move it to GPU
10  model = MyModel().cuda()
```

5.3.3 Remarks of GPU Programming via External Libraries of Prebuilt Kernel Functions

Programming GPUs, or any other kind of accelerator, by employing software libraries that implicitly use static pre-built kernels, usually offers high performance and is more productive than other solutions. However, this comes at the cost of portability due to vendor lock-in. This is because, in general, domain specific libraries are developed for particular hardware accelerators due to the requirement, in many cases, of specific hardware instructions and operations. More specifically, the software libraries are strongly dependent on the hardware vendor libraries that supply the prebuilt kernel implementations. Thus, to be able to keep up with future releases of new kernel implementations that will be designed for novel operations and may target a new generation of hardware accelerators.

The following section presents a third approach that addresses vendor lock-in by employ JIT compilation for the dynamic generation of the accelerated code.

5.4 Programming with Parallel Frameworks that Employ JIT Compilation for Heterogeneous Computing

The previous two approaches showed that using hardware accelerators (e.g., GPUs, FPGAs) from programming languages that run on an MRE can offer high performance. However, performance comes at the cost of programmability (in the case of the wrapper interfaces—Sect. 5.2) or vendor lock-in (in the case of software libraries that use pre-built kernels—Sect. 5.3). This section presents a third approach that employs transparent compilation and execution of dynamically generated kernels from a managed programming language. This approach includes frameworks that contain two fundamental components, a Just-In-Time (JIT) compiler that can dynamically generate code that runs on hardware accelerators (similar to other JIT compilers in Java and other managed languages that emit code for CPUs), and a runtime system that can automatically handle all the inner operations regarding the handling of the execution on the heterogeneous hardware. By following this approach, developers can implement their programs in one programming language (e.g., Java) and the functions that can be offloaded to accelerators are also part of those programs. Thus, the kernel functions originate from a description made using the managed language, thereby enabling developers to maintain one version of their program in the same programming language. Then, the runtime and the JIT compiler take care of the communication, compilation and data manipulation to orchestrate the execution of the whole program; as if the accelerator was part of the runtime platform (i.e., part of the physical resources accessible within the JVM).

> This approach increases the code productivity and has low maintenance cost for developers, however, it has a high engineering cost due to the work required at the compiler and runtime layers. To create a compiler and runtime system that will be smart enough to detect and compile a user program and run it on a suitable accelerator, significant effort is required to alleviate the challenges due to automatic memory management (Sect. 4.3.4) and the sophisticated compilation chains (Sect. 4.3.2), at the lowest possible performance penalty.

5.4.1 Programming Frameworks that use JIT Compilation for Heterogeneous Computing

The majority of the frameworks that belong to this category are research endeavors aiming to address the challenges that heterogeneous programming models pose to MREs (Sect. 4.3). Regarding the Python programming environment, Copperhead [78] is a high-level data parallel embedded language for Python.

Copperhead defines a subset of Python 2.6 that can be compiled and offloaded on a CUDA device (i.e., an NVIDIA GPU). It defines a set of Python decorators (i.e., annotations that can inject and modify code in Python functions) in the source code which is compiled to run on the GPU. Copperhead is a source-to-source compiler that translates, at runtime, a Python function to a CUDA kernel. It exploits parallelism through a set of primitives defined in the Python language, such as map and reduce.

Similarly to Copperhead, Numba [79] is a JIT optimizing compiler for the Python programming language. Similar to Copperhead, Numba also uses annotations (in the form of Python decorators) in the source code to give more information to the compiler regarding the optimizations that can be applied. Numba exposes a Python decorator to express that the annotated code should be used for generating CUDA kernel to run on a GPU (@cuda.jit). Numba decorators for GPUs can also define the data type of the input and output as well as the thread selection for launching the kernel. The annotated Python code that will run on the GPU is similar to the level of CUDA C and OpenCL C. FastR-GPU [101] exploits parallel constructs within the programming language to run computing intensive tasks on GPUs.

In the Java context, the project Sumatra [76] was an early OpenJDK proposal undertaken by Oracle and AMD to offload certain methods (e.g., forEach) of the Java 8 Stream API on GPUs. Additionally, AMD proposed Aparapi [77] that offers a new Java API for programming GPU kernels. The Aparapi API exposes a new type called Kernel used by developers to define the source code of a kernel, and subsequently the Aparapi compiler translates the methods to OpenCL C. Thus, this API requires developers to have a good understanding of the OpenCL programming model and know how to write a parallel computation in OpenCL C (Sect. 3.4.1**). TornadoVM [47, 81] is another Java framework for programming Java programs that can run on heterogeneous hardware. Unlike Aparapi, TornadoVM includes an optimizing JIT compiler and a runtime system that can generate kernels from Java methods at runtime, and run them on multi-core CPUs, GPUs and FPGAs. Additionally, the JIT compiler contains three backends that can generate at runtime OpenCL C, CUDA PTX, and SPIR-V binaries. To the best of our knowledge, TornadoVM is the state-of-the-art framework regarding programming applications for hardware acceleration without requiring the developers to think as implementing a code in OpenCL or CUDA.

In a nutshell, the aforementioned frameworks present the following key characteristics:

- **Performance**: Although these frameworks are considered to deliver a faster and more productive way to program, they usually achieve lower performance than other hand-tuned and ad-hoc solutions, such as wrapper interfaces and libraries using prebuilt kernels. The reason is that there is a cost due to the automatic data handling (e.g., some data marshalling between different object layouts might be required) and automatic code generation of the kernel functions (e.g., OpenCL C, CUDA, SPIR-V, SYCL, etc.).

- **Extraction of parallelism**: Programming languages running on top of MREs have not been implemented to support heterogeneous hardware execution by design. Thus, these frameworks need to extract, somehow, parallelism from the user programs in order to transform the programs to valid parallel implementations.

(continued)

- **Interactions with the GC**: Similarly to the first and second approaches, handling memory management (e.g., data allocation, manipulation and movement) in an automatic way is a sensitive process due to the GC.
- **Language Definition**: While managed programming languages offer a rich set of language constructs (e.g., inheritance, lambda expressions, exceptions, etc.), not all of them can be executed by an accelerator. Thus, the providers of those frameworks must define a subset of the features of those programming language that is supported. Similar work has been done in the C++ domain with the SYCL [82] parallel programming model.

Thus, the following section will discuss how to accelerate Java programs on GPUs with TornadoVM.

5.4.2   Programming with TornadoVM

TornadoVM is a parallel programming framework that can execute Java methods on hardware accelerators. To program a Java program with TornadoVM, a developer can use the TornadoVM APIs to perform three steps:

1. **Express parallelism in the Java methods**: This step instructs the JIT compiler regarding the generation of the parallel kernel implementations. TornadoVM exposes two APIs, the *Loop API* that exposes Java annotations to express parallelism in loops (*data-level parallelism*); and the *Kernel API* that exposes the functionality of the heterogeneous programming models to Java via the `KernelContext` object. Developers can use those APIs interchangeably, or combine them. The Loop API is recommended for programmers that are not experts in heterogeneous programming of GPUs/FPGAs. The Kernel API is recommended for experts in heterogeneous programming that require more control (e.g., accessing the thread ids, local memory, barriers, etc.).
2. **Define the methods that will be offloaded on an accelerator along with the required input/output data**: Each of those methods is defined in TornadoVM as a `task`, and developers can create a graph with multiple tasks (multiple methods) to be accelerated on the same device using the `TaskGraph` data structure. For each graph, developers also add the data needed to execute each of the tasks. By using the `TaskGraph` API, developers create a chain of methods to be accelerated. Depending on the device to be executed (e.g., an FPGA), this explicit chain of methods can be used to exploit the *pipeline-parallelism* of the entire task-graph. Besides, the `TaskGraph` data structure facilitates the TornadoVM runtime system the lookup of the methods and objects (data) to be accelerated and offloaded respectively. The `TaskGraph` data structure is also a convenient representation because it is used by the runtime to perform data-

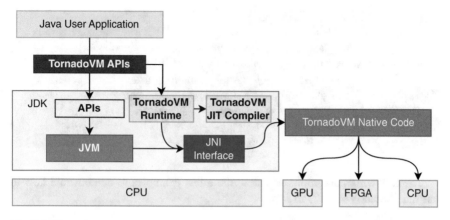

Fig. 5.3 Key software components of TornadoVM, and how they interact in the JVM

flow optimizations, and it can persist the data on the device memory if needed to save the cost of redundant data transfers between the host and the accelerator. Furthermore, two or more tasks that belong to the same `TaskGraph` can run concurrently on different hardware accelerators (*task-level parallelism*) [23].
3. **Define an execution plan regarding how the methods will be executed**: An execution plan is defined in TornadoVM as `TornadoExecutionPlan` and can configure the runtime parameters for the accelerator, such as selecting a specific device, passing different thread-block sizes, enabling batch processing, and enabling the profiler [38].

Figure 5.3 shows a diagram with the key components of TornadoVM and how they interact in the JVM. Once programmers have followed the three steps to adapt their Java program to use the TornadoVM APIs, the rest of the work is done at runtime. The TornadoVM runtime system is the core component that performs the memory management (i.e., data allocation, data transfers, etc.), the code generation via the JIT compiler, the device assignment, and the execution. The TornadoVM runtime system also communicates with the TornadoVM native code that implements inner operations (e.g., the buffer allocation, data transfers, launching of a kernel, etc.) based on the execution model of the heterogeneous programming models. Hence, Java developers implement their application using Java objects (i.e., `TaskGraph`, `TornadoExecutionPlan`) to identify and express how their program should execute on hardware accelerators, while the TornadoVM runtime system layer abstracts low-level operations that are required by heterogeneous programming models.

TornadoVM enables developers to express parallelism via its API at three levels: task-level, data-level and pipeline-level. Additionally, TornadoVM uses single-source property, as the accelerated code and the host code live in the same Java program. There is no distinction, at the source code level, between the code of a TornadoVM task and the remaining of the program. This way of programming has benefits, such as catching syntax errors at the time the main Java program is compiled.

The following paragraphs will describe a few examples to demonstrate how to use the TornadoVM APIs in Java.

5.4.3　Example of Programming Vector Multiplication with TornadoVM

This section describes a Java program that wants to offload the vector multiplication of a vector with itself on a GPU. As mentioned in previous paragraph, TornadoVM applies hardware acceleration of Java applications at the method-level. Therefore, the first step is to express the parallelism in the method body. Listing 5.30 shows the original method body that implements the vector multiplication in Java to run sequential on a CPU thread.

Listing 5.30 Java example expressed in TornadoVM to compute the square vector on GPUs

```
1  private static void computeSquare(float[] input, float[] output) {
2      for (int i = 0; i < input.length; i++) {
3          output[i] = input[i] * input[i];
4      }
5  }
```

Step 1. Express Parallelism with TornadoVM

Choice 1. Use the Loop API

The first thing that developers should consider is to analyze the method body and check if there is any data dependency [90]. As shown in Listing 5.30, all the elements of the vector are compute iteratively (line 2) and they do not have any data dependency (line 3). Thus, potentially, we could assign each iteration of that loop to be executed by a GPU thread. To do so, TornadoVM offers two Java annotations: **@Parallel** and **@Reduce**. The former annotation is used to annotate loops, whereas the latter annotation is used to define variables used for reduction operations (i.e., to accumulate values in a variable). In this example, we can annotate the for-loop with the **@Parallel** annotation to indicate to the TornadoVM JIT compiler that each iteration of the loop can run in parallel. This annotation is similar to the annotations used in OpenMP [91] and OpenACC [92]. Listing 5.31 shows the code snippet of the annotated Java method (line 2). If the annotation is not used, the TornadoVM JIT compiler will emit a kernel implementation to run on a single GPU thread.

Listing 5.31 Java example expressed in TornadoVM to compute the square vector on GPUs

```
1  private static void computeSquare(float[] input, float[] output) {
2      for (@Parallel int i = 0; i < input.length; i++) {
3          output[i] = input[i] * input[i];
4      }
5  }
```

Choice 2. Use the Kernel API

As mentioned in Sect. 5.4.2, TornadoVM also offers the Kernel API to express parallelism in a Java method. This API exposes functionality similar to OpenCL, and therefore developers can express in their methods thread-ids, local memory, barriers, etc. Listing 5.32 the code snippet of the Java method that uses the TornadoVM Kernel API to compute the vector multiplication in parallel. Note that a new argument, the context of type KernelContext (line 2), is added in the method. This type belongs to the Kernel API, and it enables developers to express thread-ids, allocation in the local memory, barriers, etc. Subsequently, we remove the declaration of the loop, and we replace the induction variable (i in Listing 5.31) to be the thread identifier (idx in Listing 5.32) that corresponds to a GPU thread. Note, that this type of replacement is common in OpenCL as discussed in Sect. 3.5.1. Finally, line 4 expresses the computation that is going to be performed by each GPU thread. Since the input and output arrays have the same size and there is no data dependency between the iterations, the same thread identifier can be used to access the data of both arrays.

Listing 5.32 Java example expressed in TornadoVM to compute the square vector on GPUs

```
1  private static void computeSquare(float[] input, float[] output,
2                                     KernelContext context) {
3      int idx = context.globalIdx;
4      output[idx] = input[idx] * input[idx];
5  }
```

Step 2. Define the Methods To Be Offloaded on an Accelerator and their Input/Output Data

Once the Java methods have been modified to express parallelism, developers must proceed to the second step. This step requires developers to create a `TaskGraph` and define which methods should be added as TornadoVM tasks in order to be compiled for accelerators. A `TaskGraph` can contain one or multiple tasks, which can be executed concurrently [23] as long as they do not have data dependency. Otherwise, the TornadoVM runtime detects the data dependency and schedules the tasks to be executed consecutively.

Listing 5.33 shows the code snippet that creates a TornadoVM `TaskGraph` object for the annotated task in Listing 5.31. A `TaskGraph` has a string name (e.g., `"compute"`) given by the developer (line 1). The name is used to query runtime information (e.g., profiling information) for a particular task, or to change the accelerator device on which the tasks of the `TaskGraph` are going to be executed. Note that in this book, we use the TornadoVM API defined in the v0.15.2 version. Future releases may alter the API and introduce new methods or deprecate some methods.

Listing 5.33 TornadoVM `TaskGraph` for to identify the `computeSquare` Java method to be offloaded and accelerated

```
1  TaskGraph taskGraph =  new TaskGraph("compute");
2  taskGraph.transferToDevice(DataTransferMode.FIRST_EXECUTION,
        ↪inputArray)
3    .task("square", TornadoVMSquare::computeSquare, inputArray,
        ↪outputArray)
4    .transferToHost(DataTransferMode.EVERY_EXECUTION, outputArray
        ↪);
```

Lines 2 and 4 define the data that to be transferred from the host (i.e., Java heap) to the device memory, and backwards, respectively. Note that TornadoVM, as in version 0.15, uses Java arrays which reside in the Java heap. The `transferToDevice` call also defines how often the data should be transferred by using a flag. In this example the flag used is `DataTransferMode.FIRST_EXECUTION`, which indicates the TornadoVM runtime system to transfer the data only before the first execution (read-only). Alternatively, developers can define that data should be transferred prior to every execution. This is the case that data are configured for a read/write operation. Similarly to the `transferToDevice` function call, the `transferToHost` method is also defined with a flag indicating how often the result data will be transferred from the device to the host. In this case, we specify every time (line 4). However, if developers want to reuse the `TaskGraph` and execute it multiple times, there is an option to define that data must be transferred only the first time and the results should be copied back to the host on-demand, by using the `USER_DEFINED` flag. That configuration eliminates the data transfers between the host and the device every time the `TaskGraph` is executed.

Line 3 defines the task (i.e., Java method) to be offloaded on an accelerator. The arguments specified in the task are the following. The first argument is a string that defines the name of the task, and it is used to identify a task within the `TaskGraph`. Similar to the name of the `TaskGraph`, the task name can be used to dynamically change the targeted accelerator device, and also to query the profiling information that the TornadoVM runtime system emits for a particular task. The second argument is a Java lambda expression or a reference to an existing Java method. In this example, that argument in line 3 points to the annotated method shown in Listing 5.30. The annotated function has name `computeSquare` and belongs to a Java class named `TornadoVMSquare`. The rest of the arguments correspond to the ordinary arguments of the `computeSquare` method.

> A `TaskGraph` is only used to define the tasks to run along with their input/output data. Thus, it does not launch or execute code by itself. The execution of a `TaskGraph` is explicitly performed by an execution plan, as is defined in the next step.

Step 3. Define an Execution Plan

Listing 5.34 shows the code snippet that creates an execution plan and executes it. Prior to the creation of an execution plan, a `TaskGraph` must be transformed to an immutable state (i.e., `ImmutableTaskGraph`) by invoking the `snapshot` method (line 2). This operation ensures that TornadoVM will execute only graphs that cannot be changed at runtime. If developers need to apply a change to a graph, they can modify the mutable `TaskGraph` and then take a new snapshot of the new version of the graph.

After that operation, line 5 defines the creation of a new object of type `TornadoExecutionPlan`. Once the execution plan is created, the application can launch the `TaskGraph` for execution on the accelerator by invoking the `execute` method (line 8). The first time that this method is invoked, TornadoVM will analyse the `TaskGraph`, compile all the tasks to a heterogeneous code format (e.g., OpenCL C, CUDA PTX, or SPIR-V), and run it on an accelerator. If developers do not explicitly configure the execution plan with the accelerator to run the `TaskGraph` via the `withDevice` method, the default device is used.

Listing 5.34 Creation of an execution plan in TornadoVM

```
1  // Create an Immutable Task Graph
2  ImmutableTaskGraph itg = taskGraph.snapshot();
3
4  // Create an Execution Plan from all immutable task graphs
5  TornadoExecutionPlan executionPlan = new TornadoExecutionPlan(itg);
6
7  // Execute the execution plan on the default device
8  executionPlan.execute();
```

Listing 5.35 shows the command used to run the TornadoVM example of vector multiplication from a command prompt. The `tornado` command is an alias to the `java` command along with all the Java flags, such as the location of the JNI libraries (e.g., path to the OpenCL JNI libraries) required to enable the TornadoVM framework to operate.

Listing 5.35 Execution of the Compute Vector Square Application in TornadoVM

```
1  $ tornado -cp target/examples-1.0-SNAPSHOT.jar \
2        com.book.hmrs.tornadovm.TornadoVMSquare
3  Hello TornadoVM
4  Test PASSED
```

The `tornado` command exposes to users several additional functionalities that can print information regarding the execution trace. For instance, `--threadInfo` is a flag used to list the accelerators and the number of threads, that are being deployed by a program. Another flag is the `-printKernel` which is used to print the generated code of the executed kernels in the command prompt. Listing 5.36 shows the execution trace of the command in Listing 5.35 with the `--threadInfo` and `--printKernel` flags enabled. Note that TornadoVM is configured to operate with the OpenCL backend in this example. Lines 7–43 present the generated OpenCL C kernel that is generated by the annotated Java method (Listing 5.30). Lines 45–52 present information about accelerator (RTX 2060 NVIDIA GPU) and the number of threads (100,000 threads) that have been deployed on the device. Finally, the number of threads in this example is determined by the upper bound of the loop expressed in the annotated method (i.e., `input.length` in Listing 5.31).

Listing 5.36 Execution trace of the Vector Square application in TornadoVM with some profiling information enabled

```
1  $ tornado --printKernel --threadInfo \
2      -cp target/examples-1.0-SNAPSHOT.jar \
3      com.book.hmrs.tornadovm.TornadoVMSquare
4      Hello TornadoVM
5
6      #pragma OPENCL EXTENSION cl_khr_fp64 : enable
7      __kernel void computeSquare(__global long *_kernel_context,
8      __constant uchar *_constant_region,
9      __local uchar *_local_region,
```

```
10        __global int *_atomics,
11        __global uchar *input,
12        __global uchar *output)
13        {
14          float f_9, f_12, f_10;
15          ulong ul_0, ul_1, ul_11, ul_8;
16          long l_6, l_5, l_7;
17          int i_13, i_2, i_4, i_3;
18
19          // BLOCK 0
20          ul_0  = (ulong) input;
21          ul_1  = (ulong) output;
22          i_2  = get_global_size(0);
23          i_3  = get_global_id(0);
24          // BLOCK 1 MERGES [0 2 ]
25          i_4  = i_3;
26          for(;i_4 < 100000;)
27          {
28            // BLOCK 2
29            l_5  = (long) i_4;
30            l_6  = l_5 << 2;
31            l_7  = l_6 + 24L;
32            ul_8  = ul_0 + l_7;
33            f_9  = *((__global float *) ul_8);
34            f_10  = *((__global float *) ul_8);
35            ul_11  = ul_1 + l_7;
36            f_12  = f_9 * f_10;
37            *((__global float *) ul_11)  = f_12;
38            i_13  = i_2 + i_4;
39            i_4  = i_13;
40          }  // B2
41          // BLOCK 3
42          return;
43        }  // kernel
44
45        Task info: compute.square
46              Backend           : OPENCL
47              Device            : NVIDIA GeForce RTX 2060
                    ↪CL_DEVICE_TYPE_GPU (available)
48              Dims              : 1
49              Global work offset: [0]
50              Global work size  : [100000]
51              Local  work size  : [1000, 1, 1]
52              Number of workgroups  : [100]
53        Test PASSED
```

5.4.4   Example of Programming Matrix Multiplication with TornadoVM and Performance Evaluation

This section presents a more complex example that shows the implementation of a matrix multiplication with TornadoVM. Listing 5.37 presents the code snippet of a Java method that is modified with the TornadoVM API to implement a parallel implementation of the canonical matrix multiplication (O^3 algorithm version). Remember that the sequential Java implementation of that computation was presented earlier in Listing 5.18 (Sect. 5.2.2). As shown in Listing 5.37, each iteration of the two outermost loops can be computed independently (i.e., no data dependencies). Therefore, we used the Loop API and annotated the first two loops with the @Parallel annotation (lines 5–6).

> Note that the @Parallel annotation can be used in a maximum depth of up to three nested loops. The reason is that it follows the supported low-level heterogeneous programming models (i.e., OpenCL, CUDA, etc.) which can abstract 1D, 2D and 3D and map to the physical hardware, computations of maximum three dimensions. Besides, multi-dimensional kernel representation is a programming abstraction that facilitates parallel programming of computing kernels. The corresponding drivers and hardware will map multi-dimensional representation into a 1D representation.

Additionally, in this example we used some data types offered by the TornadoVM collection. In this example, we defined the input and output matrices to use two dimensions via type `Matrix2DFloat` (lines 1–3). If you recall the matrix multiplication example in JOCL(Sect. 5.2.3), we discussed already this matter and decided to used matrices flattened in one dimension. In this example with TornadoVM we selected the `Matrix2DFloat` type, which is internally represented by a one-dimensional flattened matrix.

Note that if the annotated Java method presented in Listing 5.37 is invoked by a JVM as any other Java method, it will run on a Java thread and produce correct result. Whereas, if it is executed via the TornadoVM TornadoExecutionPlan (after creating an ImmutableTaskGraph), it would be compiled to a parallel implementation and executed on an accelerator.

Listing 5.37 Java code annotated with the TornadoVM API for the canonical Matrix Multiplication

```
1   private static void matrixMultiplication(Matrix2DFloat matrixA,
2                                            Matrix2DFloat matrixB,
3                                            Matrix2DFloat matrixC) {
4       // Annotated Sequential Implementation
5       for (@Parallel int i = 0; i < matrixA.getNumRows(); i++) {
6           for (@Parallel int j = 0; j < matrixB.getNumRows(); j++) {
```

```
 7              float sum = 0.0f;
 8              for (int k = 0; k < matrixC.getNumRows(); k++) {
 9                  sum += matrixA.get(i, k) * matrixB.get(k, j);
10              }
11              matrixC.set(i, j, sum);
12          }
13      }
14  }
```

Once the method is modified to express parallelism, the following steps correspond to the definition of the TaskGraph (Step 2) and the TornadoExecutionPlan (Step 3). The code snippet of those steps is presented in Listing 5.38 and is similar to the one explained in the previous example. The only difference is that in this example we enable the TornadoVM profiler (line 13). The profiler tracks information such as the kernel execution time, the time spent in data transfers, the compilation time and even the dispatch time (i.e., the elapsed time between a command being enqueued in a command queue till it is finally processed). The TornadoVM profiler has two configurations. It can display all metrics during the execution time in the command prompt using the CONSOLE flag, or it can store all metrics internally silently using the and dump the ProfilerMode.SILENT flag (as in line 13). In the latter case, the metrics can be accessed by a Java program through a new object (TornadoExecutionResult) as shown in lines 16–17. This object keeps information of every time that a TaskGraph is executed.

Listing 5.38 Java code annotated with the TornadoVM API for the canonical Matrix Multiplication

```
 1  TaskGraph taskGraph = new TaskGraph("compute");
 2  taskGraph.transferToDevice(DataTransferMode.EVERY_EXECUTION,
        ↪matrixA, matrixB)
 3      .task("mxm", TornadoVMMxM::matrixMultiplication, matrixA,
            ↪matrixB, matrixC)
 4      .transferToHost(DataTransferMode.EVERY_EXECUTION, matrixC);
 5
 6  // Create an Immutable Task Graph
 7  ImmutableTaskGraph itg = taskGraph.snapshot();
 8
 9  // Create an Execution Plan from all immutable task graphs
10  TornadoExecutionPlan executionPlan = new TornadoExecutionPlan(itg
        ↪);
11
12  // Execute the application on the default accelerator
13  executionPlan.withProfiler(ProfilerMode.SILENT);
14  // This is a blocking call,
15  // and it blocks until the kernel execution has finished.
16  TornadoExecutionResult executionResult = executionPlan.execute();
17  long kernelTime = executionResult.getProfilerResult().
        ↪getDeviceKernelTime();
18  parallelTotalTimers[i] = kernelTime;
19  System.out.print("Parallel Kernel Time (ns) = " +
        ↪parallelTotalTimers[i]);
```

Performance Evaluation

This paragraph aims to compare the TornadoVM implementation of matrix multi-plication against the Java sequential implementation and the JOCL implementation described in Sect. 5.2.3. In particular, the matrix multiplication program runs the execution plan and the Java sequential implementation for the same matrix size (1024 × 1024) that was used in the performance evaluation of the JOCL imple-mentation. Listing 5.39 presents the application trace of the program for multiple iterations and reports the execution time of the TornadoVM parallel implementation and the sequential implementation. The accelerator card is an NVIDIA RTX 2060 GPU, which is the same device used to run the JOCL implementation.

Listing 5.39 Java code annotated with the TornadoVM API for the canonical Matrix Multiplica-tion

```
1  $ tornado \
2  -cp target/examples-1.0-SNAPSHOT.jar com.book.hmrs.tornadovm.
     ↪TornadoVMMxM
3
4  Parallel Kernel Time (ns) = 5550560    Java Sequential Time (ns)
     ↪ = 1604815678
5  Parallel Kernel Time (ns) = 5548032    Java Sequential Time (ns)
     ↪ = 1635521358
6  Parallel Kernel Time (ns) = 5553856    Java Sequential Time (ns)
     ↪ = 1588632160
7  Parallel Kernel Time (ns) = 5552288    Java Sequential Time (ns)
     ↪ = 1547463370
8  Parallel Kernel Time (ns) = 5562464    Java Sequential Time (ns)
     ↪ = 1585996483
9  Parallel Kernel Time (ns) = 5027872    Java Sequential Time (ns)
     ↪ = 1775200066
10 Parallel Kernel Time (ns) = 6199296    Java Sequential Time (ns)
     ↪ = 1761014252
11 Parallel Kernel Time (ns) = 5558112    Java Sequential Time (ns)
     ↪ = 1814780312
12 Parallel Kernel Time (ns) = 6005344    Java Sequential Time (ns)
     ↪ = 1880669974
13 Parallel Kernel Time (ns) = 6536704    Java Sequential Time (ns)
     ↪ = 1705495203
14 Parallel Kernel Time (ns) = 7645824    Java Sequential Time (ns)
     ↪ = 1753107439
15 Parallel Kernel Time (ns) = 6809312    Java Sequential Time (ns)
     ↪ = 1786081736
16 Parallel Kernel Time (ns) = 5567744    Java Sequential Time (ns)
     ↪ = 1821192363
17 Parallel Kernel Time (ns) = 5986144    Java Sequential Time (ns)
     ↪ = 1816148364
18 Parallel Kernel Time (ns) = 7297024    Java Sequential Time (ns)
     ↪ = 1710566145
19 TornadoVM TIMERS
20 Min     : 5027872
21 Max     : 7645824
```

```
22   Average : 6026705.066666666
23   Variance: 5.1250865136526215E11
24   STD     : 715897.0955139168
25
26
27   JAVA TIMERS
28   Min     : 1547463370
29   Max     : 1880669974
30   Average : 1.7191123268666666E9
31   Variance: 1.0009976117217854E16
32   STD     : 1.0004986815192638E8
33
34   Result is correct
```

The execution time of both implementations is reported in nanoseconds. The execution trace in Listing 5.39 shows that the TornadoVM implementation presents an average performance speedup of 285× against to the Java sequential implementation. If we compare the parallel implementation of the TornadoVM implementation against the JOCL implementation, one expects them to achieve similar performance. However, the performance comparison between TornadoVM and JOCL shows that the TornadoVM implementation is 12.2× faster than JOCL.

The reason lies in the fact that TornadoVM is more than just a translator from Java to OpenCL or CUDA and SPIR-V [93]. It also optimizes the code. Therefore, to be able to compare properly the TornadoVM and the JOCL implementations, we need to apply the optimizations in the JOCL kernel implementation, too. After analyzing the OpenCL C code emitted by the TornadoVM JIT compiler, we saw that the main optimization applied, is loop-interchange [90]. That optimization interchanges the order of the nested loops (i.e., the two parallel annotated loops are interchanged), thereby improving the data locality in the GPU memory. Hence, that is the source of the performance difference between the two parallel implementations.

Based on the above, we can draw some conclusions. Developers that use the wrapper interfaces (first approach) are responsible for providing kernel implementations that are optimized. This is not necessarily bad; however, developers must be aware of the complexities that this approach entails. On the other hand, the frameworks described in this category make use of an optimizing JIT compiler, such as TornadoVM JIT compiler. This alleviates that burden by automatically generating fast kernel implementations. Nonetheless, in most of the cases the generated kernels will not reach the performance of hand-tuned optimized code provided by hardware vendor libraries.

5.4.5   Remarks of Programming with Parallel Frameworks that Use JIT Compilation

In this section we have explored programmability and performance of Java programs using parallel programming frameworks and JIT compilation that are able to offload part of the applications to GPUs. This approach fully abstracts away the architectural details of accelerators from the development process, and it usually offers higher code portability compared to other approaches. Ideally, the same code that can run on a standard MRE (e.g., in the JVM for the Java programming language) can be executed on the various heterogeneous hardware accelerators adhering to the "write-once-run-everywhere" paradigm that led the design of the various MREs. This also increases productivity, since developers are not required to know low-level hardware details about the GPU execution models, or even the usual GPU programming models, such as OpenCL or CUDA. Besides, code portability can be also applied across different types oh hardware accelerators. For example, in the case of TornadoVM, the same application can be executed on GPUs, FPGAs or any other type of compatible accelerator.

However, code portability and increased productivity may come at a performance cost. In general, this approach does not offer the performance that other ad-hoc solutions provide, such as hand-tuned wrapper kernels or pre-built libraries. However, technologies based on JIT compilation are continuously evolving pushing the performance boundaries, with the ultimate goal of getting closer to native solutions in terms of performance.

5.5   Implementation of Reductions with JOCL and TornadoVM

The previous sections presented the three main approaches that programmers can follow to use hardware acceleration from managed languages. To showcase the advantages and disadvantages of the programming frameworks and libraries that align with each approach, we presented in previous sections examples that implement a matrix multiplication or vector operations. In this section, we aim to showcase the implementation of a more complex example that regards the computation of a reduction operation. A reduction [69, 70] is a function that is used to accumulate a set of values into a scalar value. Examples of reduction operations are a summation, multiplication, maximum and minimum computations, etc.

In this section, we focus on programming a parallel implementation of a `summation` with the first and third approach, since reductions are not exposed by the software libraries of the second approach. Section 5.5.1 presents a vanilla Java implementation of a reduction. Section 5.5.2 describes the main considerations to create parallel implementations of reductions in OpenCL. Finally, the last two sections present the implementation of parallel reductions in Java with JOCL (Sect. 5.5.3) and TornadoVM (Sect. 5.5.4), respectively.

5.5.1   Programming Reductions in Java

To explain how to produce parallel implementations of reductions in Java, it is necessary to show first, a vanilla Java implementation of a reduction. Listing 5.40 shows a sketch code in Java that describes how to perform a summation of an input vector (line 4). As we can see, the outcome is stored in a scalar value (output) that is computed based on all the elements of the input vector. As shown in line 4, the iterative computation presents a data dependency since all the elements are added to the same value. Although this data dependency could be considered as a factor that indicates that a parallel implementation is not feasible, as we will see in the next sections, several parallel implementations have been designed.

Listing 5.40 Sequential implementation of a reduction in Java

```
1   float[] input = ...
2   float output = input[0];
3   for (int i = 1; i < input.length; i++) {
4       output += input[i];
5   }
```

5.5.2   Programming Parallel Implementations of Reductions

There have been many endeavors to create parallel implementations of reductions on GPUs [73]. The most common approach uses the *divide-and-conquer* model which splits the input vector into several groups of values. Each group can be computed in parallel by the GPU threads (i.e., partial reductions), while values that belong to the same group are computed sequentially [72, 73]. Those implementations can take advantage of further hardware optimizations, such as the allocation of data in local memory (or shared memory), the deployment of multiple blocks of threads that can run independently, etc.

> It is out of the scope of this book to implement the fastest implementation of reductions. The example in this book aims to show the considerations required for programming parallel implementation of reductions from managed languages.

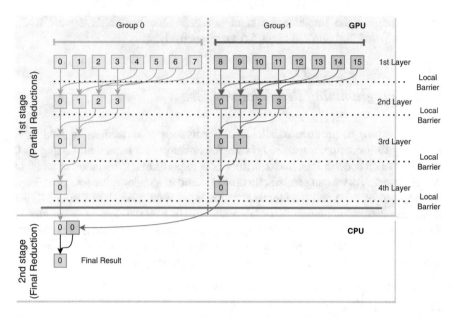

Fig. 5.4 Example of how to compute parallel reductions in OpenCL

Figure 5.4 shows the workflow of the GPU threads to compute a parallel reduction in OpenCL. The reduction operation is separated in two stages. The first stage corresponds to the partial reductions which are simultaneously executed on a GPU, while the second stage refers to the final reduction that runs on a CPU and accumulates the results of the partial reductions into one scalar value. As shown in Fig. 5.4, the partial reductions are executed in four layers. In the first layer, the input vector shown in this figure contains 16 integer elements and it is processed in parallel by two groups (Group 0 and Group 1) of eight GPU threads. Subsequently, the second layer launches the same kernel to process the result produced at the previous layer. Thus, the GPU threads deployed per group in the second layer are four. The same procedure is followed for every following layer. Consequently, the last layer (layer 4) computes the final partial reduction on the GPU. Once the partial reductions have been executed on the GPU, the second stage is launched on the CPU to compute the final reduction.

If the size of the input vector is too large to be processed by the number of physical GPU threads, an OpenCL kernel will be launched as many times as needed until all data are processed within a work group. Note that a similar workflow will be observed for parallel reductions implemented in other heterogeneous programming models, such as CUDA, SYCL, and Intel oneAPI.

As shown in Fig. 5.4, the input elements are grouped in pairs during the dividing of the input vector. To take advantage of data locality, the elements within a work group can be copied in the local memory (i.e., CUDA shared memory). That step can result in fast memory accesses for the GPU threads that belong to the same work group. However, it is necessary to synchronize the data stored in local memory after the completion of the processing in a layer. The synchronization is performed by adding a local barrier as a fence to the GPU threads.

> As mentioned in Sect. 2.7.6, the local memory of GPUs is not coherent. Thus, developers are responsible for explicitly adding barriers to synchronize the GPU threads when accessing data in local memory (Sect. 3.4.1).

5.5.3 Programming Reductions with JOCL

At this stage, it is time to create a parallel implementation of a reduction with JOCL. Listing 5.41 presents the code snippet of an OpenCL kernel that processes a reduction in parallel. Line 1 stores the kernel implementation in a string type. The kernel has three arguments in the following order, the input array, the output array that will store the results of the partial reductions, and a pointer to a region (localSums) allocated in the local memory of the GPU.

Listing 5.41 Sum reduction kernel in JOCL

```
1   private static String openCLReductionProgram =
2   "__kernel void "+
3   "reduce(__global const float *input," +
4   "        __global float *partialSums," +
5   "        __local float *localSums)" +
6   "{ "+
7   "    uint idx = get_global_id(0);" +
8   "    uint localIdx = get_local_id(0);" +
9   "    uint group_size = get_local_size(0);" +
10  "    localSums[localIdx] = input[idx]; " +
11  "    for (int stride = group_size/2; stride > 0; stride /= 2) {"+
12  "        barrier(CLK_LOCAL_MEM_FENCE);" +
13  "        localSums[localIdx] += localSums[localIdx + stride];"+
14  "    } "+
15  "    if (localIdx == 0) {"+
16  "        partialSums[get_group_id(0)] = localSums[0]; " +
17  "    }; "+
18  "}";
```

Line 10 copies the data from the global memory of the device to the local memory that is declared in the third argument of the kernel. Thus, the localSums array can be shared by all GPU threads that belong to the same work group. However, since the data in this array can be written by many GPU threads, developers must explicitly add a local barrier right before loading the data from local memory (line 12). The barrier acts as a guarantee that all threads will be synchronized, and they will have the same view of the local memory right after the barrier. Line 13 performs the partial reduction which is executed simultaneously by the GPU threads of each work group. Finally, lines 15–17 copy the results of the partial reductions from the local memory to the global memory. After the completion of the kernel, the data pointed by the partialSums pointer contain the results of all parallel partial reductions. Then, in the host side, developers must perform a final reduction over those partial results to obtain the final result.

Listing 5.42 presents the code snippet for setting the kernel arguments before launching the kernel on an accelerator. The interesting part is that the memory size of the local memory region that will be used by the kernel, is declared at this stage, as shown in line 7. This way the size of the local memory region used in the kernel is declared dynamically, and a change of the size in line 7 will not require the kernel to be recompiled.

Listing 5.42 Kernel arguments for the kernel shown in Listing 5.41

```
1  // Set the arguments for the kernel
2  int argId = 0;
3  CL.clSetKernelArg(kernel, argId++, Sizeof.cl_mem, Pointer.to(
       ↪deviceBufferInput));
4  CL.clSetKernelArg(kernel, argId++, Sizeof.cl_mem, Pointer.to(
       ↪deviceBufferOutput));
5
6  // Local Memory declaration
7  CL.clSetKernelArg(kernel, argId++, Sizeof.cl_float * 256, null);
```

Listing 5.43 shows the trace of the execution of the kernel on an NVIDIA RTX 3070 GPU and a CPU (Intel 12th Gen Intel(R) Core(TM) i7-12700K at 3.60 GHz [74]). There are two key remarks from the inspection of the execution trace:

1. The execution of the Java method on a CPU thread takes shorter time than the JOCL implementation that runs on an NVIDIA RTX 3070 GPU.
2. The standard deviation of the OpenCL kernel time is larger than the standard deviation of the Java execution time.

That performance behavior is studied in other works [72] and it is attributed to the small data size and the unoptimized kernel implementation. Those factors in combination with the fact that the OpenJDK JIT compiler (HotSpot C2 JIT compiler) can vectorize the code result in the Java implementation outperforming a parallel GPU implementation. Additionally, due to small input sizes, GPUs usually do not run at the highest frequency without tuning the driver parameters [75].

Listing 5.43 Kernel Execution Timers for the OpenCL kernel executed with JOCL versus the Java execution time for the reduction application

```
1  ----------------------------------
2  Using OpenCL platform: NVIDIA CUDA
3  Device Name: NVIDIA GeForce RTX 3070
4  ----------------------------------
5  Parallel Kernel Time (ns) = 23360        Java Sequential Time (ns)
       ↪ = 6300
```

```
 6  Parallel Kernel Time (ns) = 11232      Java Sequential Time (ns)
        ↪ = 6200
 7  Parallel Kernel Time (ns) = 7168       Java Sequential Time (ns)
        ↪ = 5701
 8  Parallel Kernel Time (ns) = 6144       Java Sequential Time (ns)
        ↪ = 5500
 9  Parallel Kernel Time (ns) = 23264      Java Sequential Time (ns)
        ↪ = 5601
10  Parallel Kernel Time (ns) = 5920       Java Sequential Time (ns)
        ↪ = 5301
11  Parallel Kernel Time (ns) = 21856      Java Sequential Time (ns)
        ↪ = 5699
12  Parallel Kernel Time (ns) = 5952       Java Sequential Time (ns)
        ↪ = 5700
13  Parallel Kernel Time (ns) = 21472      Java Sequential Time (ns)
        ↪ = 5600
14  Parallel Kernel Time (ns) = 6144       Java Sequential Time (ns)
        ↪ = 5599
15  Parallel Kernel Time (ns) = 18592      Java Sequential Time (ns)
        ↪ = 5600
16  Parallel Kernel Time (ns) = 18464      Java Sequential Time (ns)
        ↪ = 5599
17  Parallel Kernel Time (ns) = 19264      Java Sequential Time (ns)
        ↪ = 5600
18  Parallel Kernel Time (ns) = 7040       Java Sequential Time (ns)
        ↪ = 5501
19  Parallel Kernel Time (ns) = 7168       Java Sequential Time (ns)
        ↪ = 5600
20  OpenCL program finished
21
22  JOCL TIMERS
23  Min      : 5920
24  Max      : 23360
25  Average : 13536.0
26  Variance: 5.0627925333333336E7
27  STD      : 7115.330303881426
28
29
30  JAVA TIMERS
31  Min      : 5301
32  Max      : 6300
33  Average : 5673.4
34  Variance: 60559.573333333334
35  STD      : 246.08854774924683
36
37  Result is correct
```

This section has described how to use the local memory of GPUs and how to program using local thread indexes (indexes within an OpenCL work group) in order to access data. Furthermore, it analyzed the performance of two reductions implementations, the JOCL parallel implementation and the Java sequential implementation.

A key takeaway of this sections is that there are several factors that can impact the performance of parallel implementations against optimizing JIT compilers, such as the HotSpot JIT compiler, that can emit vector instructions.

5.5.4 Programming Reductions with TornadoVM

This section presents a parallel implementation of a reduction with the TornadoVM API. Additionally, it will show a performance comparison of that implementation against the JOCL implementation described in the previous section. To be fair the same reduction (summation) is implemented for both systems.

Listing 5.44 presents the code snippet of the annotated Java method that was presented earlier in Listing 5.40. The @Parallel annotation is used in the loop (line 2) and the @Reduce annotation is used in line 1 to declare the scalar value that will store the result of the reduction. In this case, the loop is considered parallel despite the fact that there is a data dependency. The reason is that the TornadoVM runtime system recognizes that data dependency and knows how to satisfy it in order to generate a parallel implementation.

Listing 5.44 Simple sum reduction in Java and TornadoVM

```
1  private static void reduction(float[] input, @Reduce float[]
       ↪output) {
2      for (@Parallel int i = 0; i < input.length; i++) {
3          output[0] += input[i];
4      }
5  }
```

In reality, the TornadoVM runtime system performs code analysis prior to any inner operation (e.g., compilation or allocation of device buffers). The objective of the code analysis in TornadoVM is to detect patterns, such as reductions, and re-write the application at runtime. By rewriting the applications at runtime TornadoVM can automatically apply all changes needed to process a full parallel reduction (i.e., both partial reductions and the final reduction). Once TornadoVM detects a reduction operation in the code, it splits the method into two kernel implementations. One kernel performs the parallel processing of the partial reductions on the GPU, similar to the one explained in the JOCL implementation (Sect. 5.5.3). The second kernel performs the final reductions over the results of the partial reductions and is executed again on the GPU with one thread. The main reason that TornadoVM launches also the second kernel on the GPU, instead of processing on the host, is to avoid transferring the result of the partial reductions. Thus, the final result of the GPU execution is a single value that contains the result of the reduction.

Listing 5.45 presents the `TaskGraph` implementation that contains one task for the `reduction` method (lines 2–5). Additionally, lines 8–11 show the steps of transforming the `TaskGraph` to an immutable state and creating an execution plan. Finally, line 14 configures the execution plan to use the TornadoVM profiler in the silent mode during the execution.

Listing 5.45 TornadoVM `TaskGraph` and Execution Plan for the Reduction Example

```
1  // Create TornadoVM TaskGraph
2  TaskGraph taskGraph = new TaskGraph("compute");
3  taskGraph.transferToDevice(DataTransferMode.FIRST_EXECUTION,
       ↪inputArray)
4           .task("reduce", TornadoVMReduction::reduction, inputArray
                 ↪, outputArray)
5           .transferToHost(DataTransferMode.EVERY_EXECUTION,
                 ↪outputArray);
6
7  // Create an Immutable Task Graph
8  ImmutableTaskGraph itg = taskGraph.snapshot();
9
10 // Create an Execution Plan from all immutable task graphs
11 TornadoExecutionPlan executionPlan = new TornadoExecutionPlan(itg
       ↪);
12
13 // Enable profiler metrics
14 executionPlan.withProfiler(ProfilerMode.SILENT);
```

If we launch the application to compute a reduction over 1024 elements, we see the kernel information shown in Listing 5.46. Note that TornadoVM has separated the annotated method (`reduction` in Listing 5.44) into two kernels: one parallel (`reduction`—same name as the Java method) that performs the partial reductions on 1024 GPU threads, and one sequential (`rAdd`) that accumulates the final result.

Listing 5.46 Execution trace of the Reduction example implemented in TornadoVM

```
1  $ tornado --printKernel --threadInfo \
2     -cp target/examples-1.0-SNAPSHOT.jar \
3     com.book.hmrs.tornadovm.TornadoVMReduction
4
5  #pragma OPENCL EXTENSION cl_khr_fp64 : enable
6  #pragma OPENCL EXTENSION cl_khr_int64_base_atomics : enable
7  __kernel void reduction(...)
8  {
9     bool b_25, b_18;
10    int i_24, i_23, i_20, i_16, i_15, i_17, i_14, i_13, i_7, i_4,
         ↪i_3;
11    int i_6, i_5, i_33, i_28, i_27;
12    long l_8, l_9, l_10, l_31, l_29, l_30;
13    float f_21, f_22, f_19, f_26, f_12;
14    ulong ul_1, ul_0, ul_32, ul_11;
15
16    // BLOCK 0
17    ul_0  =  (ulong) input;
```

```
18    ul_1  =  (ulong) output;
19    __local float adf_2[256];
20    i_3  =  get_global_size(0);
21    i_4  =  get_global_id(0);
22    // BLOCK 1 MERGES [0 11 ]
23    i_5  =  i_4;
24    for(;i_5 < 1024;)
25    {
26      // BLOCK 2
27      i_6  =  get_local_id(0);
28      i_7  =  get_local_size(0);
29      l_8  =  (long) i_5;
30      l_9  =  l_8 << 2;
31      l_10  =  l_9 + 24L;
32      ul_11  =  ul_0 + l_10;
33      f_12  =  *((__global float *) ul_11);
34      adf_2[i_6]  =  f_12;
35      i_13  =  i_7 >> 31;
36      i_14  =  i_13 + i_7;
37      i_15  =  i_14 >> 1;
38      // BLOCK 3 MERGES [2 7 ]
39      i_16  =  i_15;
40      for(;i_16 >= 1;)
41      {
42        // BLOCK 4
43        barrier(CLK_LOCAL_MEM_FENCE);
44        i_17  =  i_16 >> 1;
45        b_18  =  i_6 < i_16;
46        if(b_18)
47        {
48          // BLOCK 5
49          f_19  =  adf_2[i_6];
50          i_20  =  i_16 + i_6;
51          f_21  =  adf_2[i_20];
52          f_22  =  f_19 + f_21;
53          adf_2[i_6]  =  f_22;
54        }  // B5
55        else
56        {
57          // BLOCK 6
58        }  // B6
59        // BLOCK 7 MERGES [6 5 ]
60        i_23  =  i_17;
61        i_16  =  i_23;
62      }  // B7
63      // BLOCK 8
64      barrier(CLK_GLOBAL_MEM_FENCE);
65      i_24  =  i_3 + i_5;
66      b_25  =  i_6 == 0;
67      if(b_25)
68      {
69        // BLOCK 9
70        f_26  =  adf_2[0];
71        i_27  =  get_group_id(0);
```

```
72        i_28  =  i_27 + 1;
73        l_29  =  (long) i_28;
74        l_30  =  l_29 << 2;
75        l_31  =  l_30 + 24L;
76        ul_32  =  ul_1 + l_31;
77        *((__global float *) ul_32)  =  f_26;
78      }  // B9
79      else
80      {
81        // BLOCK 10
82      }  // B10
83      // BLOCK 11 MERGES [10 9 ]
84      i_33  =  i_24;
85      i_5  =  i_33;
86    }  // B11
87    // BLOCK 12
88    return;
89  }  // kernel
90
91  Task info: XXX__GENERATED_REDUCE0.reduce
92          Backend          : OPENCL
93          Device           : NVIDIA GeForce RTX 2060
                 ↪CL_DEVICE_TYPE_GPU (available)
94          Dims             : 1
95          Global work offset: [0]
96          Global work size  : [1024]
97          Local  work size  : [256, 1, 1]
98          Number of workgroups  : [4]
99
100
101  #pragma OPENCL EXTENSION cl_khr_fp64 : enable
102  #pragma OPENCL EXTENSION cl_khr_int64_base_atomics : enable
103  __kernel void rAdd(...)
104  {
105    float f_6, f_4, f_10, f_8, f_13, f_14, f_11, f_12, f_2;
106    ulong ul_1, ul_0, ul_9, ul_7, ul_5, ul_3;
107
108    // BLOCK 0
109    ul_0  =  (ulong) array;
110    ul_1  =  ul_0 + 24L;
111    f_2  =  *((__global float *) ul_1);
112    ul_3  =  ul_0 + 28L;
113    f_4  =  *((__global float *) ul_3);
114    ul_5  =  ul_0 + 32L;
115    f_6  =  *((__global float *) ul_5);
116    ul_7  =  ul_0 + 36L;
117    f_8  =  *((__global float *) ul_7);
118    ul_9  =  ul_0 + 40L;
119    f_10  =  *((__global float *) ul_9);
120    f_11  =  f_2 + f_4;
121    f_12  =  f_11 + f_6;
122    f_13  =  f_12 + f_8;
123    f_14  =  f_13 + f_10;
124    *((__global float *) ul_1)  =  f_14;
```

```
125    return;
126  } // kernel
127
128  Task info: XXX__GENERATED_REDUCE0.reduce_seq0
129          Backend            : OPENCL
130          Device             : NVIDIA GeForce RTX 2060
                  ↪CL_DEVICE_TYPE_GPU (available)
131          Dims               : 0
132          Global work offset: [0]
133          Global work size   : [1]
134          Local  work size   : [1, 1, 1]
135          Number of workgroups  : [1]
```

Listing 5.47 presents the full application trace that runs both the kernels generated by TornadoVM and the Java sequential code. We observe similar behavior with the JOCL kernel implementation. The execution time of both kernels does not outperform the sequential Java code for this data size (1024 elements). Nonetheless, there are works showing that the TornadoVM implementations of other applications that compute reductions (e.g., integral approximation or PI computation approximation) can outperform the Java sequential implementations [72].

Listing 5.47 Execution trace of the Reduction example implemented in TornadoVM

```
1  $ tornado \
2  -cp target/examples-1.0-SNAPSHOT.jar com.book.hmrs.tornadovm.
       ↪TornadoVMReduction
3  WARNING: Using incubator modules: jdk.incubator.vector, jdk.
       ↪incubator.concurrent
4  Parallel Kernel Time (ns) = 22848      Java Sequential Time (ns)
       ↪ = 11090
5  Parallel Kernel Time (ns) = 11872      Java Sequential Time (ns)
       ↪ = 15867
6  Parallel Kernel Time (ns) = 10912      Java Sequential Time (ns)
       ↪ = 23474
7  Parallel Kernel Time (ns) = 10208      Java Sequential Time (ns)
       ↪ = 11000
8  Parallel Kernel Time (ns) = 10848      Java Sequential Time (ns)
       ↪ = 14275
9  Parallel Kernel Time (ns) = 11648      Java Sequential Time (ns)
       ↪ = 10102
10 Parallel Kernel Time (ns) = 10912      Java Sequential Time (ns)
       ↪ = 10753
11 Parallel Kernel Time (ns) = 11360      Java Sequential Time (ns)
       ↪ = 10677
12 Parallel Kernel Time (ns) = 10240      Java Sequential Time (ns)
       ↪ = 16231
13 Parallel Kernel Time (ns) = 11776      Java Sequential Time (ns)
       ↪ = 16437
14 Parallel Kernel Time (ns) = 10688      Java Sequential Time (ns)
       ↪ = 10720
15 Parallel Kernel Time (ns) = 10816      Java Sequential Time (ns)
       ↪ = 10394
```

```
16  Parallel Kernel Time (ns) = 10880        Java Sequential Time (ns)
        ↪ = 10625
17  Parallel Kernel Time (ns) = 10816        Java Sequential Time (ns)
        ↪ = 10475
18  Parallel Kernel Time (ns) = 10240        Java Sequential Time (ns)
        ↪ = 23184
19  JOCL TIMERS
20  Min      : 10208
21  Max      : 22848
22  Average : 11737.6
23  Variance: 9075124.906666666
24  STD      : 3012.494797782507
25
26
27  JAVA TIMERS
28  Min      : 10102
29  Max      : 23474
30  Average : 13686.933333333332
31  Variance: 1.926238286222222E7
32  STD      : 4388.89312494873
33
34  Result is correct
```

5.6 Summary

This chapter aimed to bind the heterogeneous programming models and the managed programming languages that have been discussed in the last two chapters. Thus, it described three approaches that programmers can follow to program heterogeneous hardware from programming languages that run on top of an MRE. Additionally, it demonstrated code snippets of examples, and highlighted the pros and cons of each approach. We hope that the reader should have a notion of how to program hardware accelerators from managed programming languages such as Java and Python, and how/when to use each approach. Readers will find supplementary exercises to reflect on the material discussed in this chapter [17].

Chapter 6
Conclusions

6.1 Mission, Contents and Contributions

This book aimed to introduce to the reader how heterogeneous hardware acceleration is changing the programming landscape, while posing a number of challenges
to existing programming languages. In particular, the focus of this book has
been on dynamic programming languages executed on top of managed runtime
environments. After having introduced heterogeneous hardware acceleration and
explained why it has become prevalent in modern computing systems (Chap. 2), we
elaborated on the programmings models that are currently being used to program
such accelerators (Chap. 3). For simplicity, our discussions were focused mainly on
a particular class of heterogeneous hardware accelerators; that of General Purpose
GPUs. GPUs have become increasingly important due to their high performance and
suitability for AI/ML workloads across different application domains. Nevertheless,
both the discussion on heterogeneous programming models and the challenges
they pose on MREs are transferable across different hardware accelerators and
programming models.

After having introduced the fundamental characteristics of the various heterogeneous programming models that are currently being used (Chap. 3), we diverted
the discussion on MREs by outlining their key architectural components (Chap. 4).
Through this discussion, we explained the particular challenges that MREs face
when trying to integrate them with the current standard heterogeneous programming
models. The discussion over those challenges aimed to illuminate how current
solutions, of accelerating applications running on top of MREs, operate and why
they differ amongst them regarding their architecture and capabilities (Chap. 5). At
the time of writing this book, enriching current MREs with capabilities to exploit
hardware accelerators is an evolving endeavor with constant innovations from both
industry and academia.

© The Author(s), under exclusive license to Springer Nature Switzerland AG 2024   127
J. Fumero et al., *Programming Heterogeneous Hardware via Managed
Runtime Systems*, SpringerBriefs in Computer Science,
https://doi.org/10.1007/978-3-031-49559-5_6

6.2   Current and Future Trends

Despite the ongoing innovations, a number of early conclusions that may or may not materialize in future systems can be drawn. Regarding code generation, a combination of JIT-compiled code and usage of pre-built kernels is foreseen [43]. Although highly optimized pre-built kernels, typically provided by hardware vendors in the form of libraries, such as cuBLAS [33], oneDNN [34], cuDNN [36], etc., yield the highest performance, automatically generated kernels via JIT compilation assist in exploring high performance implementations of new algorithms at a faster pace. To this end, novel extensions to traditional managed programming languages have been introduced to enable such functionality (e.g., TornadoVM [47, 50], Mojo [51]). In such solutions, performance is driven both by the quality of the compiler and the developers' expertise in exploiting low-level heterogeneous programming primitives in their code [38]. In these hybrid models, a key element for high performance is the fast transitions between the managed language and the various native functions. Hence, extensive research is performed and new innovative solutions are currently being introduced in various managed programming languages; e.g., Project Panama [83], Alibaba fastFFI [84], Python Bindings [39], etc.

Regarding memory management, the current standard solution is the usage of off-heap memory; with new evolving projects currently being brought into the market assisting the easy creation and manipulation of off-heap memory either in raw form [83] or via off-heap data structures [85]. However, recent research works started exploring the possibility of using unified shared memory in combination with proposed GC extensions in order to directly access data stored in the heap from heterogeneous hardware accelerators [89].

Regardless of how the programming language landscape will evolve in the upcoming years, a certain fact is that programming languages will be extended to embrace heterogeneous hardware accelerators into their execution models. Thankfully, in most cases the consolidation and uniformity of such innovations are governed by standard bodies in an effort to enable performance portability across devices of different vendors (e.g., Khronos group [86], the newly founded UXL Foundation [87], PyTorch Foundation [88], OpenJDK via the newly proposed Babylon project,[1] and others).

Regardless of how programming languages will be shaped in the future, a certain fact is that we, the developers, shall start learning how to exploit the capabilities of heterogeneous hardware accelerators. This book aimed to provide an introduction towards this endeavor along with offering a set of practical examples towards learning GPU programming. Happy coding!

---

[1] https://mail.openjdk.org/pipermail/discuss/2023-September/006226.html.

References

1. Tor M. Aamodt, Wilson Wai Lun Fung, and Timothy G. Rogers. 2018. General-purpose Graphics Processor Architectures. Morgan & Claypool Publishers.
2. DirectX Graphics and Gaming. Microsoft. URL last accessed in September 2023: https://learn.microsoft.com/en-gb/windows/win32/directx
3. OpenGL. URL last accessed in September 2023: https://www.opengl.org/.
4. Vulkan 1.3.265 - A Specification (with all registered Vulkan extensions). The Khronos Vulkan Working Group. URL last accessed in September 2023: https://registry.khronos.org/vulkan/specs/1.3-extensions/pdf/vkspec.pdf.
5. GeForce 256. URL last accessed in September 2023: https://en.wikipedia.org/wiki/GeForce_256
6. John Nickolls, David Kirk. Graphics and Computing GPUs. Appendinx B from Computer Organization and Design, Fifth Edition: The Hardware/Software Interface.
7. Fortune Business Insights. GPU as a Service Market. URL last accessed in September 2023: https://www.fortunebusinessinsights.com/gpu-as-a-service-market-107797
8. Laurent LefebvreAndrew E. GruberStephen L. Morein. Multi-thread graphics processing system. Patent US7742053B2. https://patentimages.storage.googleapis.com/5f/a8/3b/6d357236a6fb9b/US7742053.pdf
9. Ian Buck, Tim Foley, Daniel Horn, Jeremy Sugerman, Kayvon Fatahalian, Mike Houston, and Pat Hanrahan. 2004. Brook for GPUs: stream computing on graphics hardware. ACM Trans. Graph. 23, 3 (August 2004), 777–786. https://doi.org/10.1145/1015706.1015800
10. Intel. Hitting the Shelves: Intel Arc A750 and A770 GPUs Release Today!. Press release. URL last accessed in September 2023: https://game.intel.com/story/intel-arc-graphics-release/
11. Intel. White paper: Introduction to the Xe-HPG Architecture.
12. NVIDIA. What Is NVLink? URL last accessed in September 2023: https://blogs.nvidia.com/blog/2023/03/06/what-is-nvidia-nvlink/
13. OpenAI - AI and Compute. URL last accessed in September 2023: https://openai.com/research/ai-and-compute
14. Exercises relevant to Chapter 2. URL last accessed in October 2023: https://github.com/ProgrammingHMREs/code-examples-hmre-book/blob/main/chapter2/Exercises.md
15. Exercises relevant to Chapter 3. URL last accessed in October 2023: https://github.com/ProgrammingHMREs/code-examples-hmre-book/blob/main/chapter3/Exercises.md
16. Exercises relevant to Chapter 4. URL last accessed in October 2023: https://github.com/ProgrammingHMREs/code-examples-hmre-book/blob/main/chapter4/Exercises.md

© The Author(s), under exclusive license to Springer Nature Switzerland AG 2024
J. Fumero et al., *Programming Heterogeneous Hardware via Managed Runtime Systems*, SpringerBriefs in Computer Science,
https://doi.org/10.1007/978-3-031-49559-5

17. Exercises relevant to Chapter 5. URL last accessed in October 2023: https://github.com/ ProgrammingHMREs/code-examples-hmre-book/blob/main/chapter5/Exercises.md

18. Wikipedia Moore's Law. URL last accessed in September 2023: https://en.wikipedia.org/ wiki/Moore's_law

19. Moore, Gordon E (1965) Cramming more components onto integrated circuits. Electronics volume 38, number 8.

20. R.H. Dennard, F.H. Gaensslen, Hwa-Nien Yu, V.L. Rideout, E. Bassous, and A.R. LeBlanc (1974) Design of ion-implanted mosfet's with very small physical dimensions. IEEE Journal of Solid-State Circuits, 9(5):256–268.

21. Graves, Catherine (2019) High Performance, Power Efficient Hardware Accelerators: Emerging Devices, Circuits and Architecture Co-Design. Association for Computing Machinery, doi: https://doi.org/10.1145/3310273.3324055

22. James Clarkson, Juan Fumero, Michail Papadimitriou, Maria Xekalaki, Christos Kotselidis (2018) Towards practical heterogeneous virtual machines. Conference Companion of the 2nd International Conference on Art, Science, and Engineering of Programming, page 46–48, doi: https://doi.org/10.1145/3191697.3191730

23. Michail Papadimitriou, Eleni Markou, Juan Fumero, Athanasios Stratikopoulos, Florin Blanaru, Christos Kotselidis (2021) Multiple-Tasks on Multiple-Devices (MTMD): Exploiting Concurrency in Heterogeneous Managed Runtimes. 17th ACM SIGPLAN/SIGOPS International Conference on Virtual Execution Environments, pages 125-138, doi: https://doi.org/10. 1145/3453933.3454019

24. JVenners, B (1998) Inside the Java Virtual Machine. Computing McGraw-Hill, isbn: 9780079132482

25. Microsoft Common Language Runtime. URL last accessed in September 2023: https://learn. microsoft.com/en-us/dotnet/standard/clr?redirectedfrom=MSDN

26. Python Software Foundation - The Python programming language. URL last accessed in September 2023: https://www.python.org

27. Intel®Corporation - Intel®64 and IA-32 Architectures Software Developer Manuals. URL last accessed in September 2023: https://www.intel.com/content/www/us/en/developer/ articles/technical/intel-sdm.html

28. ARM A64 Instruction Set Architecture. URL last accessed in September 2023: https:// developer.arm.com/Architectures/A64%20Instruction%20Set%20Architecture

29. JTianqi Chen, Thierry Moreau, Ziheng Jiang, Lianmin Zheng, Eddie Yan, Haichen Shen, Meghan Cowan, Leyuan Wang, Yuwei Hu, Luis Ceze, Carlos Guestrin, and Arvind Krishnamurthy (2018) TVM: An automated end-to-end optimizing compiler for deep learning. 13th USENIX Symposium on Operating Systems Design and Implementation (OSDI 18), pages 578–594, isbn: 978-1-939133-08-3

30. Francois Chollet et al. Keras. URL last accessed in September 2023: https://keras.io

31. Oracle Corporation GraalVM. URL last accessed in September 2023: https://www.graalvm. org

32. JRuby. URL last accessed in September 2023: https://www.jruby.org

33. cuBLAS: Basic Linear Algebra on NVIDIA GPUs. URL last accessed in September 2023: https://docs.nvidia.com/cuda/cublas/index.html

34. Intel oneAPI Deep Neural Network Library. URL last accessed in September 2023: https:// www.intel.com/content/www/us/en/developer/tools/oneapi/onednn.html

35. Intel oneAPI Math Kernel Library. URL last accessed in September 2023: https://www.intel. com/content/www/us/en/developer/tools/oneapi/onemkl.html

36. NVIDIA CUDA Deep Neural Network library. URL last accessed in September 2023: https:// developer.nvidia.com/cudnn

37. AMD Vitis Accelerated Libraries. URL last accessed in September 2023: https://github.com/ Xilinx/Vitis_Libraries

38. TornadoVM Programming Model. URL last accessed in September 2023: https://tornadovm. readthedocs.io/en/latest/programming.html

39. Python Bindings: Calling C or C++ From Python. URL last accessed in September 2023: https://realpython.com/python-bindings-overview/

40. Oracle Corporation - GraalVM Truffle. URL last accessed in September 2023: https://www.graalvm.org/22.0/graalvm-as-a-platform/language-implementation-framework/

41. Aho, Alfred V. and Lam, Monica S. and Sethi, Ravi and Ullman, Jeffrey D. (2006) Compilers: Principles, Techniques, and Tools (2nd Edition). Addison-Wesley Longman Publishing Co., Inc., isbn: 0321486811

42. Duboscq, Gilles Marie. (2016) Combining speculative optimizations with flexible scheduling of side-effects. PhD thesis. https://epub.jku.at/urn:nbn:at:at-ubl:1-9708

43. Byungsoo Jeon, Sunghyun Park, Peiyuan Liao, Sheng Xu, Tianqi Chen, and Zhihao Jia. 2023. Collage: Seamless Integration of Deep Learning Backends with Automatic Placement. In Proceedings of the International Conference on Parallel Architectures and Compilation Techniques (PACT '22). Association for Computing Machinery, New York, NY, USA, 517–529. doi: https://doi.org/10.1145/3559009.3569651

44. Jones, Richard and Hosking, Antony and Moss, Eliot. (2023) The Garbage Collection Handbook: The Art of Automatic Memory Management (2nd Edition). Chapman & Hall/CRC, isbn: 978-1032218038

45. Adam Paszke, Sam Gross, Francisco Massa, Adam Lerer, James Bradbury, Gregory Chanan, Trevor Killeen, Zeming Lin, Natalia Gimelshein, Luca Antiga, Alban Desmaison, Andreas Kopf, Edward Yang, Zachary DeVito, Martin Raison, Alykhan Tejani, Sasank Chil- amkurthy, Benoit Steiner, Lu Fang, Junjie Bai, and Soumith Chintala (2019) Pytorch: An imperative style, high-performance deep learning library. Advances in Neural Information Processing Systems 32, pages 8024–8035, doi: https://doi.org/10.5555/3454287.3455008

46. Martín Abadi, Ashish Agarwal, Paul Barham, Eugene Brevdo, Zhifeng Chen, Craig Citro, Greg Corrado, Andy Davis, Jeffrey Dean, Matthieu Devin, Sanjay Ghemawat, Ian Goodfellow, Andrew Harp, Geoffrey Irving, Michael Isard, Yangqing Jia, Rafal Jozefowicz, Lukasz Kaiser, Manjunath Kudlur, Josh Levenberg, Dan Mané, Rajat Monga, Sherry Moore, Derek Murray, Chris Olah, Mike Schuster, Jonathon Shlens, Benoit Steiner, Ilya Sutskever, Kunal Talwar, Paul Tucker, Vincent Vanhoucke, Vijay Vasudevan, Fernanda Viégas, Oriol Vinyals, Pete Warden, Martin Wattenberg, Martin Wicke, Yuan Yu, and Xiaoqiang Zheng (2016) Tensorflow: Large-scale machine learning on heterogeneous distributed systems. USENIX Association, pages 265–283, doi: https://doi.org/10.5555/3026877.3026899

47. Juan Fumero, Michail Papadimitriou, Foivos S. Zakkak, Maria Xekalaki, James Clarkson, and Christos Kotselidis. (2019) Dynamic application reconfiguration on heterogeneous hardware. 15th ACM SIGPLAN/SIGOPS International Conference on Virtual Execution Environments, pages 165–178, doi: https://doi.org/10.1145/3313808.3313819

48. O. Segal, P. Colangelo, N. Nasiri, Z. Qian, and M. Margala. (2015) Aparapi-UCores: A High Level Programming Framework for Unconventional Cores. IEEE High Performance Extreme Computing Conference , pages 1–6, doi: https://doi.org/10.1109/HPEC.2015.7322440

49. K. Ishizaki, A. Hayashi, G. Koblents, and V. Sarkar. (2015) Compiling and Optimizing Java 8 Programs for GPU Execution. International Conference on Parallel Architecture and Compilation (PACT), pages 419-431, doi: https://doi.org/10.1109/PACT.2015.46

50. TornadoVM. URL last accessed in September 2023: https://www.tornadovm.org

51. Modular AI: Mojo. URL last accessed in September 2023: https://www.modular.com/mojo

52. NVIDIA CUDA Unified Memory Documentation. URL last accessed in September 2023: https://docs.nvidia.com/cuda/cuda-c-programming-guide/index.html#um-unified-memory-programming-hd

53. Intel Unified Shared Memory Allocations. URL last accessed in September 2023: https://www.intel.com/content/www/us/en/docs/oneapi/optimization-guide-gpu/2023-1/unified-shared-memory-allocations.html

54. J. Reinders, B. Ashbaugh, J. Brodman, M. Kinsner, J. Pennycook, and X. Tian. (2021) Data Parallel C++: Mastering DPC++ for Programming of Heterogeneous Systems using C++ and SYCL. Berkeley, CA: Apress, pp. 67–71. [Online]. Available: https://doi.org/10.1007/978-1-4842-5574-2

55. S. Chien, I. Peng, and S. Markidis. (2019) Performance Evaluation of Advanced Features in CUDA Unified Memory. IEEE/ACM Workshop on Memory Centric High Performance Computing (MCHPC). doi: https://doi.org/10.1109/MCHPC49590.2019.00014

56. R. Landaverde, Z. Tiansheng, A. K. Coskun, and M. Herbordt. (2014) An Investigation of Unified Memory Access Performance in CUDA. IEEE High Performance Extreme Computing Conference (HPEC). doi: https://doi.org/10.1109/HPEC.2014.7040988

57. N. Sakharnykh. (2017) Maximizing Unified Memory Performance in CUDA. URL last accessed in September 2023: https://developer.nvidia.com/blog/maximizing-unified-memory-performance-cuda/

58. Christopher J. Rossbach, Yuan Yu, Jon Currey, Jean-Philippe Martin, and Dennis Fetterly. 2013. Dandelion: a compiler and runtime for heterogeneous systems. In Proceedings of the Twenty-Fourth ACM Symposium on Operating Systems Principles (SOSP '13). Association for Computing Machinery, New York, NY, USA, 49–68. https://doi.org/10.1145/2517349.2522715

59. GitHub Repository of the Book Examples. URL last accessed in September 2023: https://github.com/ProgrammingHMREs/code-examples-hmre-book

60. JOCL: Java bindings for OpenCL. URL last accessed in September 2023: http://www.jocl.org/.

61. Built-in Vector Data Types in OpenCL. URL last accessed in September 2023: https://registry.khronos.org/OpenCL/specs/3.0-unified/html/OpenCL_C.html#table-builtin-vector-types.

62. Built-in Scalar Data Types in OpenCL. URL last accessed in September 2023: https://registry.khronos.org/OpenCL/sdk/1.0/docs/man/xhtml/scalarDataTypes.html

63. Operators Used in OpenCL. URL last accessed in September 2023: https://man.opencl.org/operators.html

64. Math Built-In Functions in OpenCL. URL last accessed in September 2023: https://man.opencl.org/mathFunctions.html

65. The Specification Description of the clCreateBuffer Function. URL last accessed in September 2023: https://man.opencl.org/clCreateBuffer.html

66. The Barrier Documentation in OpenCL. URL last accessed in September 2023: https://registry.khronos.org/OpenCL/sdk/1.0/docs/man/xhtml/barrier.html

67. NVIDIA CUDA Toolkit Documentation - Memory Management. URL last accessed in September 2023: https://docs.nvidia.com/cuda/cuda-runtime-api/group__CUDART__MEMORY.html

68. Java bindings for OpenCL. JOCL JNI Documentation. URL last accessed in September 2023: https://github.com/gpu/JOCL/blob/master/src/main/java/org/jocl/CL.java

69. Michael McCool, Arch D. Robison, James Reinders, Chapter 2 - Background, Editor(s): Michael McCool, Arch D. Robison, James Reinders, Structured Parallel Programming, Morgan Kaufmann, 2012, Pages 39-75, ISBN 9780124159938. https://doi.org/10.1016/B978-0-12-415993-8.00002-5.

70. Murray I. Cole. 1988. Algorithmic skeletons: a structured approach to the management of parallel computation. Ph.D. Dissertation.

71. Intel Arc A770 Graphics SPEC. URL last accessed in September 2023: https://www.intel.com/content/www/us/en/products/sku/229151/intel-arc-a770-graphics-16gb/specifications.html

72. Juan Fumero and Christos Kotselidis. 2018. Using compiler snippets to exploit parallelism on heterogeneous hardware: a Java reduction case study. In Proceedings of the 10th ACM SIGPLAN International Workshop on Virtual Machines and Intermediate Languages (VMIL 2018). Association for Computing Machinery, New York, NY, USA, 16–25. https://doi.org/10.1145/3281287.3281292

73. Mark Harris. Optimizing Parallel Reduction in CUDA. NVIDIA Developer Technology. URL last accessed in September 2023: https://developer.download.nvidia.com/assets/cuda/files/reduction.pdf.

74. Intel Core i7-12700K Processor. SPEC. URL last accessed in September 2023: https://www.intel.com/content/www/us/en/products/sku/134594/intel-core-i712700k-processor-25m-cache-up-to-5-00-ghz/specifications.html.

75. Magni, Alberto. Analysis and parameter prediction of compiler transformation for graphics processors. PhD 2016. The University of Edinburgh.

76. Project Sumatra. OpenJDK proposal for Acceleration of Java Streams on GPUs. URL last accessed in September 2023: https://openjdk.org/projects/sumatra/

77. Aparapi for GPUs. URL last accessed in September 2023: https://github.com/Syncleus/aparapi

78. Bryan Catanzaro, Michael Garland, and Kurt Keutzer. 2011. Copperhead: compiling an embedded data parallel language. In Proceedings of the 16th ACM symposium on Principles and practice of parallel programming (PPoPP '11). Association for Computing Machinery, New York, NY, USA, 47–56. https://doi.org/10.1145/1941553.1941562

79. Siu Kwan Lam, Antoine Pitrou, and Stanley Seibert. 2015. Numba: a LLVM-based Python JIT compiler. In Proceedings of the Second Workshop on the LLVM Compiler Infrastructure in HPC (LLVM '15). Association for Computing Machinery, New York, NY, USA, Article 7, 1-6. https://doi.org/10.1145/2833157.2833162

80. John Aycock, 2003. A brief history of just-in-time. In ACM Comput. Surv. 35, 2 (June 2003), 97–113. https://doi.org/10.1145/857076.857077

81. TornadoVM Source Code on GitHub. URL last accessed in September 2023: https://github.com/beehive-lab/TornadoVM.

82. SYCL Standard. URL last accessed in September 2023: https://www.khronos.org/sycl/.

83. Project Panama: Interconnecting JVM and native code. URL last accessed in September 2023: (https://openjdk.org/projects/panama/)

84. fastFFI: Modern and Efficient FFI for Java and C++. URL last accessed in September 2023: https://github.com/alibaba/fastFFI

85. NumPy: The fundamental package for scientific computing with Python. URL last accessed in September 2023: https://numpy.org

86. The Khronos Group. URL last accessed in September 2023: https://www.khronos.org

87. The UXL Foundation. URL last accessed in September 2023: https://uxlfoundation.org/

88. The PyTorch Foundation. URL last accessed in September 2023: https://pytorch.org/foundation

89. Fumero Alfonso, J, Blanaru, F, Stratikopoulos, A, Dohrmann, S, Viswanathan, S and Kotselidis, C 2023, Unified Shared Memory: Friend or Foe? Understanding the Implications of Unified Memory on Managed Heaps, In Proceedings of the 20th International Conference on Managed Programming Languages and Runtimes.

90. Ken Kennedy and John R. Allen. 2001. Optimizing compilers for modern architectures: a dependence-based approach. Morgan Kaufmann Publishers Inc., San Francisco, CA, USA.

91. OpenMP Standard. URL last accessed in September 2023: https://www.openmp.org/specifications/

92. OpenACC Standard. URL last accessed in September 2023: https://www.openacc.org/specification

93. James Clarkson, Juan Fumero, Michail Papadimitriou, Foivos S. Zakkak, Maria Xekalaki, Christos Kotselidis, and Mikel Lujan. 2018. Exploiting high-performance heterogeneous hardware for Java programs using graal. In Proceedings of the 15th International Conference on Managed Languages and Runtimes (ManLang '18). Association for Computing Machinery, New York, NY, USA, Article 4, 1-13. https://doi.org/10.1145/3237009.3237016

94. Malcolm, James G. et al. ArrayFire: a GPU acceleration platform. Defense, Security, and Sensing (2012).

95. Eli Stevens, Luca Antiga, and Thomas Viehmann. Deep Learning with PyTorch. Manning - ISBN 9781617295263.

96. Intel Processor i9 13900K Raptor Lake Processor. URL last accessed in September 2023: https://en.wikipedia.org/wiki/Raptor_Lake.
97. Liang, Sheng. The Java native interface: programmer's guide and specification. Addison-Wesley Professional, 1999.
98. Benjamin J. Evans, James Gough, and Chris Newland. 2018. Optimizing Java: Practical Techniques for Improving JVM Application Performance (1st. ed.). O'Reilly Media, Inc.
99. Scott Oaks. 2014. Java Performance: The Definitive Guide (1st. ed.). O'Reilly Media, Inc.
100. Jack Shirazi. 2002. Java Performance Tuning (2nd. ed.). O'Reilly & Associates, Inc., USA.
101. Juan Fumero, Michel Steuwer, Lukas Stadler, and Christophe Dubach. 2017. Just-In-Time GPU Compilation for Interpreted Languages with Partial Evaluation. SIGPLAN Not. 52, 7 (July 2017), 60–73. https://doi.org/10.1145/3140607.3050761
102. NVIDIA. NVIDIA ADA GPU Architecture White paper. URL last accessed in September 2023: https://images.nvidia.com/aem-dam/Solutions/geforce/ada/nvidia-ada-gpu-architecture.pdf.
103. Andy Huang. 2023. SYCLomatic compatablity library: making migration to SYCL easier. In Proceedings of the 2023 International Workshop on OpenCL (IWOCL'23). Association for Computing Machinary, New York, NY, USA, Article 5, 1–2. https://doi.org/10.1145/3585341.3585349

Printed in the United States
by Baker & Taylor Publisher Services